TREASURES OF THE
ANDES

THE GLORIES OF INCA AND PRE-COLUMBIAN SOUTH AMERICA

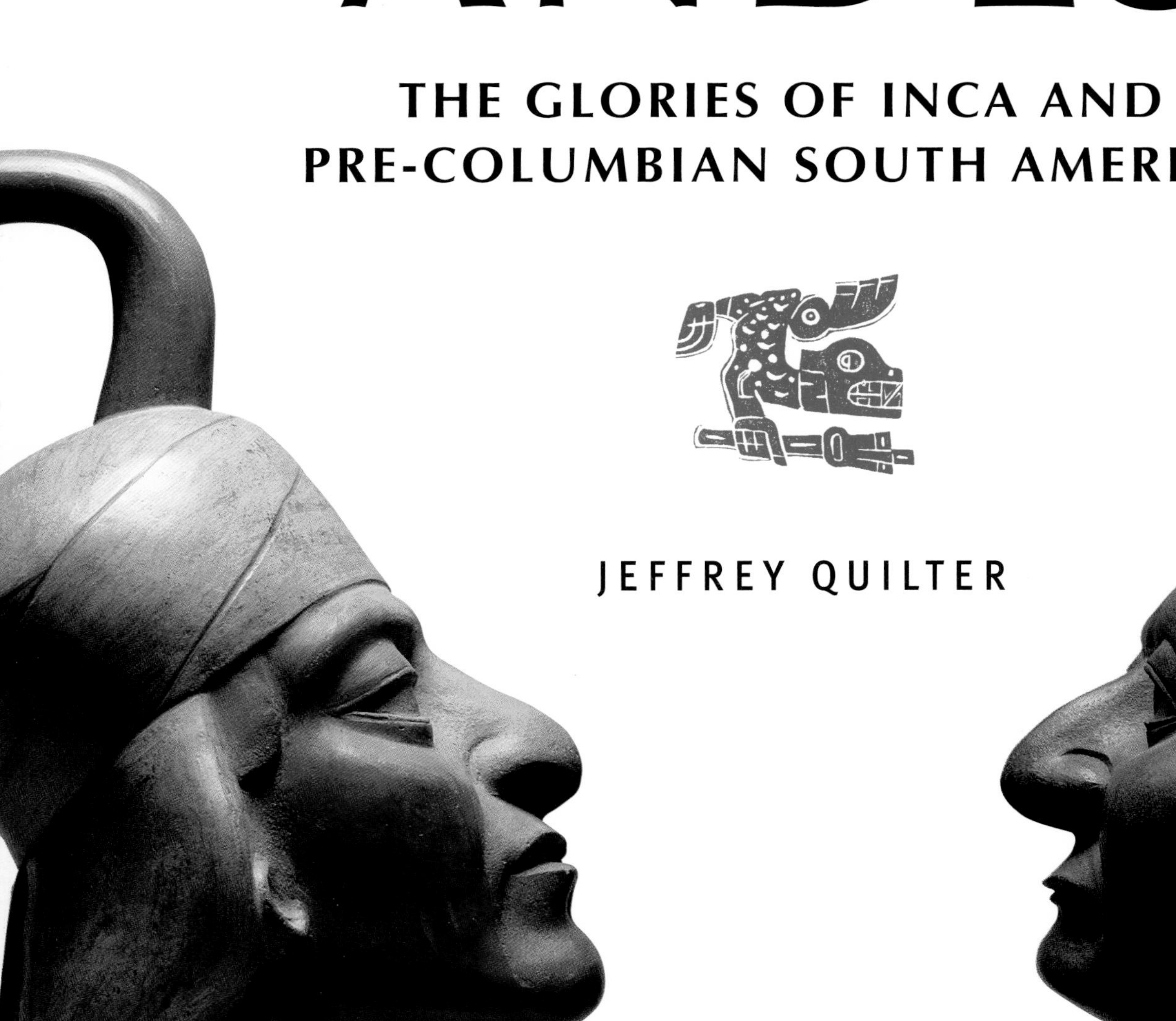

JEFFREY QUILTER

DUNCAN BAIRD PUBLISHERS
LONDON

Treasures of the Andes

First published in the United Kingdom and Ireland in 2005 by:

Duncan Baird Publishers Ltd
Sixth Floor
Castle House
75–76 Wells Street
London W1T 3QH

Conceived, created and designed by Duncan Baird Publishers

Editor: Peter Bently
Designer: Allan Sommerville
Managing Editor: Christopher Westhorp
Managing Designer: Manisha Patel
Picture Researcher: Julia Ruxton
Commissioned Artwork: Maps by Gary Walton, linocuts by Allan Sommerville

Library of Congress Cataloging-in-Publication Data is available

ISBN-10: 1-84483-217-1 ISBN-13: 9-781844-832170

10 9 8 7 6 5 4 3 2 1

Typeset in Perpetua and Optima
Colour reproduction by Scanhouse, Malaysia
Printed in Singapore by Imago

A NOTE ON DATES

CE (Common Era) and BCE (Before the Common Era) are used throughout instead of AD and BC respectively. All dates given for archaeological and cultural periods are only approximate.

To My Mother,
Joan Quilter,
Who told me to go to Peru.

CAPTIONS FOR PAGES 1–4

PAGE 1: Paracas textile with people carrying trophy heads.

PAGE 2: The foothills and snow-clad peaks of the Andes.

PAGE 3: Moche stirrup-spouted vessels in the form of human heads.

PAGE 4: A llama made of folded sheet silver inlaid with cinnabar and gold, probably to represent the red blanket of the royal (*puka*) llama. Inca-period piece from the Lake Titicaca region of Bolivia.

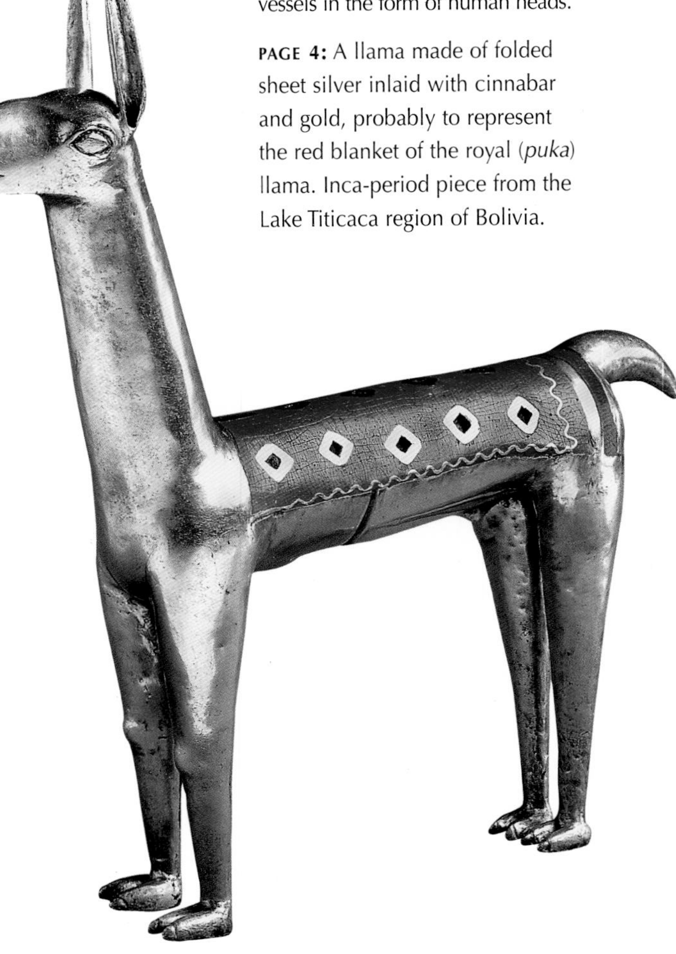

CONTENTS

INTRODUCTION

THE REALM OF INTI

OPPOSITE
Gold regalia made for a lord of the Chimú kingdom on Peru's north coast. Late Intermediate Period, ca. 1000–1450CE.

BELOW
A Moche container in the form of two birds, made of shell adorned with sheet gold and turquoise and shell inlay. The Moche, also of the north coast, flourished in the Early Intermediate Period, ca. 0CE–650CE.

The Inca who encountered the Spanish in the early sixteenth century held sway over one of the largest empires in the world, ruled by an emperor who was revered as the Son of Inti, the great Inca sun god. However, the lords of that mighty Andean realm were the inheritors of thousands of years of rich and diverse cultural traditions and innovations.

Over millennia, various cultures rose and fell in the three great environmental regions of the Andes: the tropical forest, the highlands, and the coastal desert river valleys. Throughout this time, there were periods when peoples were in greater or lesser contact with each other, and when one group was more innovative than the others. Archaeologists divide Andean prehistory broadly into seven major chronological periods, which are covered in turn by the chapters that follow. Three of these periods were times of great cultural unity and are known as the Early Horizon (ca. 700BCE to the Common Era), the Middle Horizon (ca. 650CE–ca. 1000CE), and the Late Horizon (ca. 1450–ca. 1534). These were periods when ideas and peoples of the highlands either influenced or conquered lowlanders. The Early Horizon (covered in Chapter 2) is known primarily for the spread of the Chavín cult. The Middle Horizon (Chapter 4) was the time of the Wari empire and a possible similar empire based on the city of Tiwanaku in Bolivia. The Late Horizon (Chapter 6) corresponds to the rise of the Inca, the last and greatest state built by conquest before the arrival of the Spanish in 1532 and the collapse of Inca rule.

The other periods are times of more diverse cultural patterning. The Preceramic Period (covered in Chapter 1) was the time of the arrival of the first humans to these lands and the development of the first settled communities. The Initial Period (also Chapter 1) saw the first use of pottery and woven textiles and the spread of

ABOVE
For ancient Andean peoples, the snow-capped mountains were the home of *apus*, ancestral mountain deities who, if properly respected and propitiated, would ensure the continuation of the cycle of life-sustaining water and of all the other rhythms of the cosmos.

large temple complexes throughout the Andes. The Early Intermediate Period (Chapter 3) and Late Intermediate Period (Chapter 5) were both times of complex regional cultures following the collapse of the unifying forces of Chavín, Wari and Tiwanaku respectively.

From their capital of Cuzco, in the southern highlands of the central Andes, the Inca conquered and incorporated the lands of the cultures that had preceded them: to the south, the Chilean desert and northwestern Argentina; to the east, the Bolivian *altiplano*, or plateau; to the north and west, what is now Peru and beyond through Ecuador. Only the deeper reaches of the tropical forest were not fully under Inca imperial rule, but the ancient dwellers of the jungle played a part in shaping the culture of the central Andes.

To strangers to these lands, travel seems formidable. Deserts separate the narrow strips of lush coastal river valleys. In the highlands, travelers must venture through cold mountain passes where the thin air blows in gales. The dark forests are dense and forbidding to outsiders. But these dramatically different zones, each with

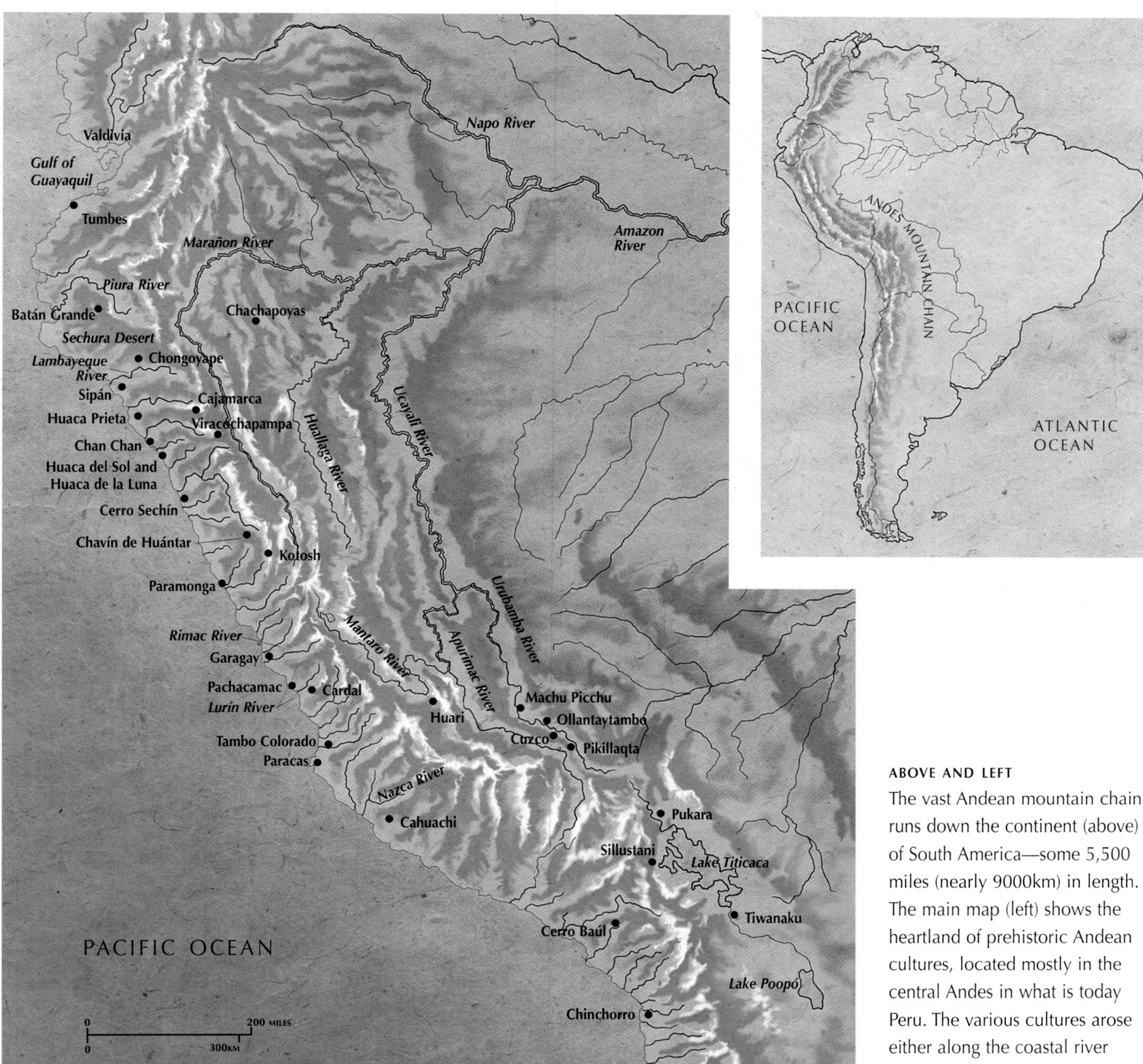

ABOVE AND LEFT
The vast Andean mountain chain runs down the continent (above) of South America—some 5,500 miles (nearly 9000km) in length. The main map (left) shows the heartland of prehistoric Andean cultures, located mostly in the central Andes in what is today Peru. The various cultures arose either along the coastal river valleys, in the fertile highlands or in the tropical lowlands.

its unique plants, animals, and other resources, are pressed close together. In ancient times, those prepared to make the effort of moving between them were rewarded with the riches offered by coast, highlands, and tropical lowlands. It was out of this richness that the grandeur of ancient Andean civilization was born.

LEFT
The variation in altitude and terrain to be found in the Andes results in a diversity of resource zones, often within close proximity of one another. This rich variety can be seen in this view near Cuzco, the old Inca capital, which shows highland plateau, valley, and, in the distance, mountain peaks.

A WEALTH OF RESOURCES

Each environmental zone of the Andes brought its own gifts of animals, plants, and minerals that provided food, shelter, and other necessities. The varied environments were also a source of luxuries, such as textiles, produced in a great range of hues, tones, and textures. The tropical forest provided colorful bird feathers, animal pelts and teeth, hardwoods, and many plants—not only foods and medicines but also mind-altering drugs. The highlands provided hard stone for tools, sculpture, and building. It offered minerals, including gold, and pasture lands for camelids (alpacas and llamas). These animals were sources of meat, but more importantly served as pack animals for transportation and provided fine wool for warm clothes and beautiful textiles.

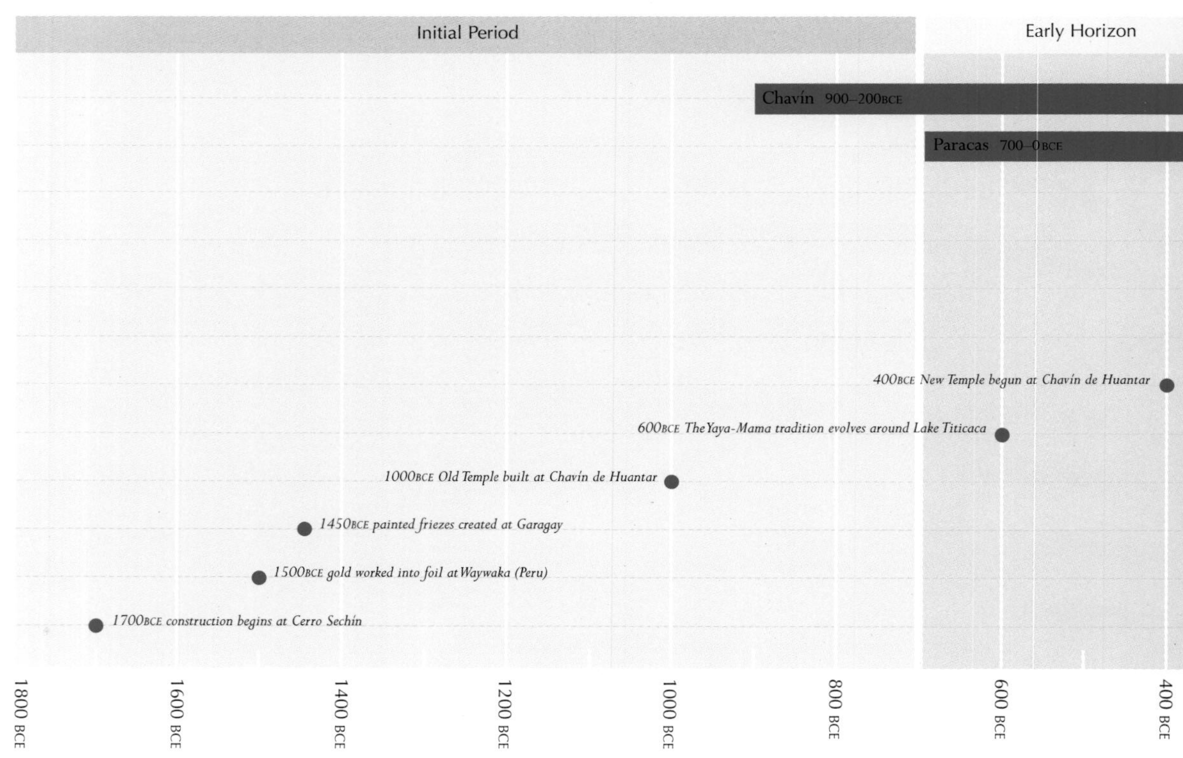

RIGHT
Dating Andean chronology and cultures is an imprecise art. The chronological periods are broadly agreed and begin with a couple of Preceramic eras: Early Preceramic (ca. 10,000–3000BCE) and Preceramic (ca. 3000–1800BCE). The dates for the rise and eclipse of cultures are more approximate, and should of course be understood to indicate not that a culture disappears from the historic record but that it had passed its peak of influence.

RIGHT
These twin Moche copper and shell owls exemplify Andean concerns with birds as spirit messengers and with the importance of pairs in a dualistic universe. (See also pages 80–81.)

Plentiful rainfall in the highland valleys ensured abundant harvests of maize at lower altitudes, quinoa and oca higher up, and potatoes and other tubers in the highest zones. Andean peoples soon learned to take full advantage of the slopes by creating well-drained terraces.

The western slopes of the Andes lie in a rain shadow and are barren. In the southern summer the heat of the coastal plain and hills pushes the clouds formed over the Pacific upward to become rain in the highlands. In the winter, with a narrower range of temperatures, the oceanic cloud drifts onto shore, producing months of overcast skies. In some places the fog blankets

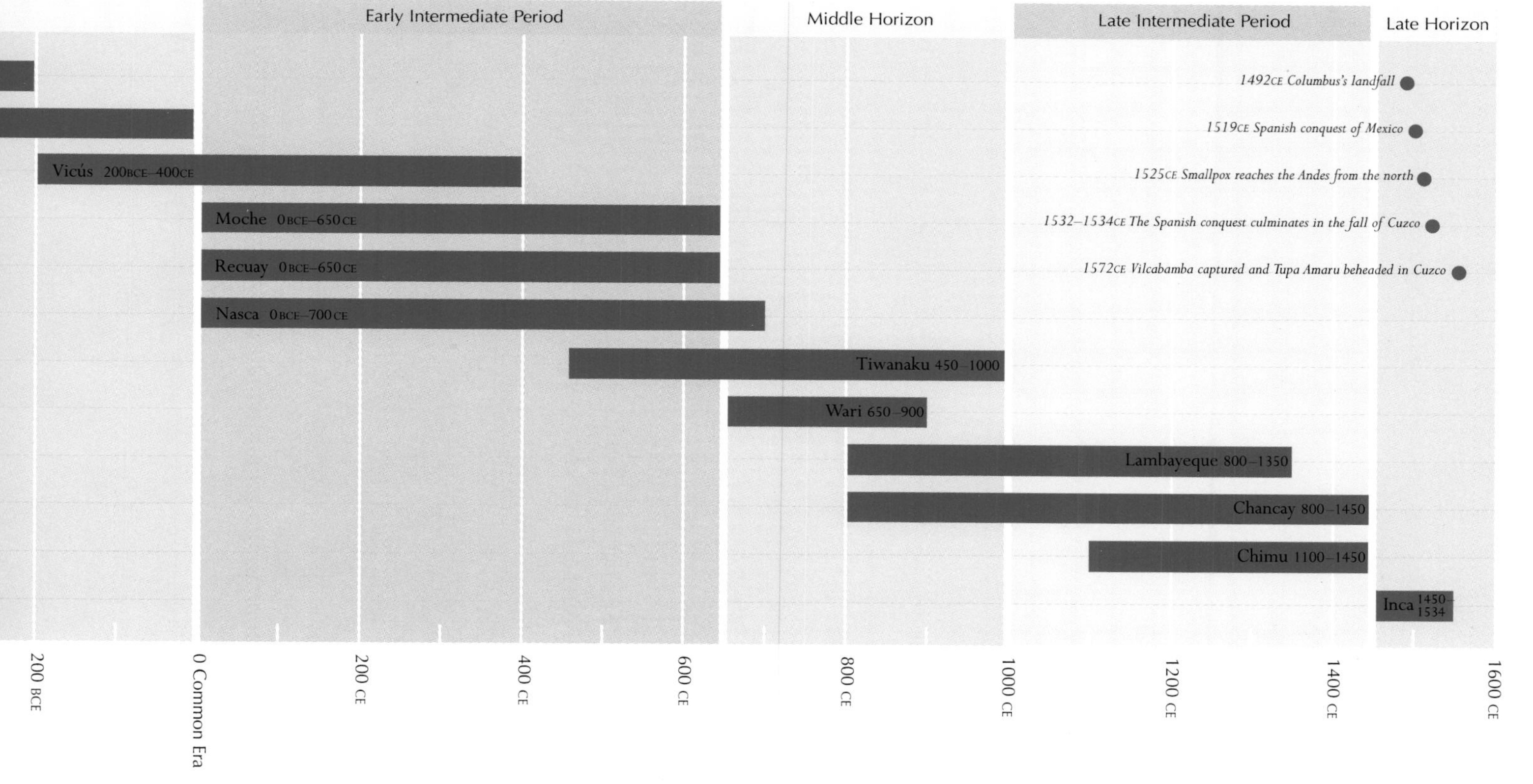

RIGHT
A fabulous bird resembling a toucan, exquisitely fashioned by a Moche artisan in sheet gold with turquoise inlay. Toucans, found farther north along the coast or across the Andes in the jungle, would have been exotic to the Moche. Andean people were keenly aware of other creatures and powerful animals were recognized as masters of their realms: the great black caiman, the jaguar, and the harpy eagle in the jungle; the puma and the hawk in the mountains; the fox and the dog on the coast; and the killer whale and other marine species in the ocean.

the hills, close to shore, and fosters the growth of a unique zone of vegetation known as *lomas*. Elsewhere, the fog passes over some of the driest land on earth, leaving at most a light film of moisture on the barren plain.

The ribbons of water that flow westward from the mountains to the sea provide oases in the desert. As the rivers descend from the heights they replicate small versions of the tropical forests on the western slopes. Closer to the sea, wide floodplains were once covered in forests and marshes for early hunters and gatherers whose farming descendants built canals with which to extend their fields.

Western South America is the home of one of the great maritime cultures of the world, based on the great riches brought by the cold Humboldt Current that runs from deep in the southern Pacific northward along the Peruvian coast. Its cold upwelling waters bring great amounts of fish such as anchovies, sardines, grouper, bonito, sea bass, and many others, as well as crustaceans, seals, walruses, and sealions.

The current swings back out to sea near the present Peru–Ecuador border as it meets warmer waters flowing southward. This countercurrent sometimes overrides the Humboldt, fostering disastrous rains on the Peruvian coast and drought in the highlands. This is the phenomenon known as El Niño (The Child), and great Andean

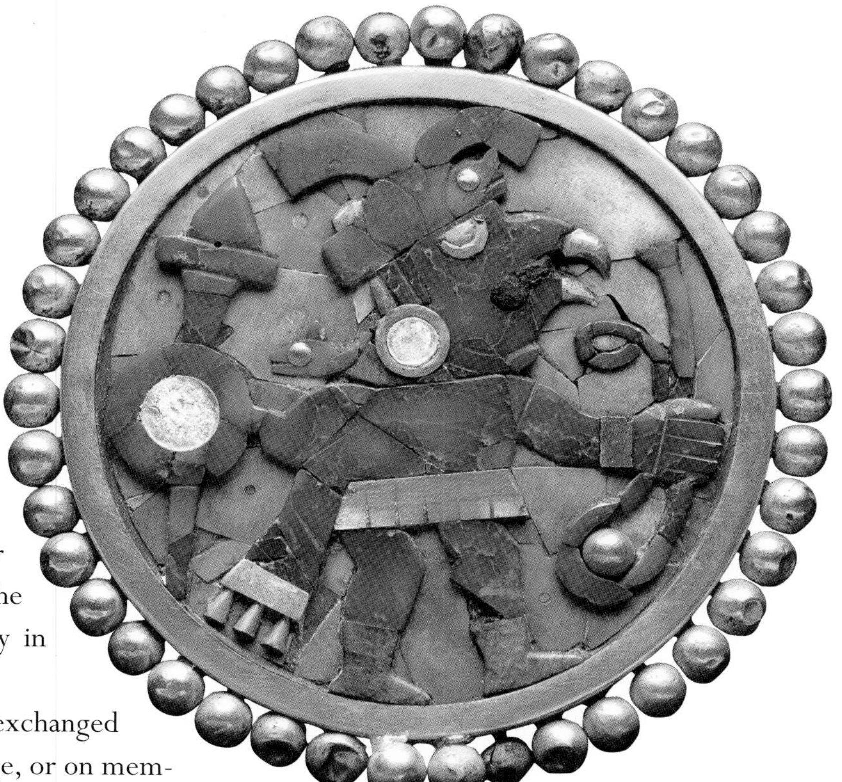

civilizations were shaken by the disruptions that it caused. The name refers to the Christ Child and is said to have originated because the first signs occur near Christmas, the southern midsummer. But the term also contains much irony, reflecting the way in which Andean child gods can bring good or ill.

Andean peoples did not use money. People exchanged goods with others based on ties of blood or marriage, or on membership of groups based on principles of dynamic, asymmetrical dualism. This concept was widespread in the ancient Americas. In some places it took the form of "Big Brother" and "Little Brother": closely related and interdependent but of slightly different status. Unsurprisingly in a land of steep hills and mountains, Andean dualism was expressed as "Upper" and "Lower," at least by the time of the Incas, whose capital, Cuzco, was divided into upper and lower sectors (see page 190).

Although no money was in circulation (except perhaps in northern Peru, for a brief period late in prehistory), some materials had very high values. Deep in the warm waters off Ecuador dwells a spiny oyster, *Spondylus princeps*, whose red shell was valued more than any other substance. Other varieties of spondylus had purple and orange shells and were valued less. It was the very food of the gods, essential for rituals, and used for the most precious ornaments and jewelry (see pages 150–153).

For the peoples of the Andes, the human world was part of a larger, cosmic dualism. Energy flowed from sea to mountains, from sky to earth, and from the human realm to that of the gods. Humans fed the gods through sacrifices and in turn were fed through the beneficence of the deities, and all of the universe revolved through fluid states of being. The practice of the Incas and their predecessors of treating mummies as if they were still alive demonstrates how life and death, too, were seen not as polar extremes but as part of a continuous flow of energies.

ABOVE
A Moche ear spool made of a mosaic of semi-precious stones, gold, and shell, with a deity warrior depicted. The beak, rendered in gold, indicates that he is an avian god or mythical creature but he is dressed as a human warrior with a club and shield in his right hand and a sling, with a golden sling stone, in his left hand.

SOURCES OF KNOWLEDGE

We know about the Andean past through many sources. The Incas were never fully conquered, and their descendants live today in the highlands of Peru, still speaking the Inca tongue, Quechua. In many places in the mountains, crops are still grown much as they were half a millennium ago, and many customs remain relatively unchanged. Because the Inca resisted the Spanish so fiercely and for so long, there was plenty of time for the invaders to observe Inca behavior and to record their beliefs and practices. From the written accounts of the Spanish we know of such phenomena as *khipu* (Inca knotted string records) and *chasqui*s (specialized runners who relayed messages across the Inca empire). Used cautiously—and bearing in mind that what the Incas told the Spanish may have been shaped by the interests of both parties—these documents offer glimpses back into the pre-contact period for a century or so.

BELOW

In 1946–47 excavations by Junius Bird in the lower Chicama River valley uncovered the earliest remains of human presence in the Andes to date at Huaca Prieta, a small fishing village occupied during the Preceramic and Initial periods (see pages 24–25). Here, an Initial Period structure of cylindrical adobes (mud bricks) is under excavation.

ABOVE
Between ca. 1587 and 1615, Felipe Guamán Poma de Ayala composed an 800-page "letter" to the Spanish king protesting at injustices to native Andean peoples. His discussion of Inca history and customs and many of the 400 illustrations he made for his manuscript have been an important source for modern scholars. The illustrations above show a girl with llamas and the Inca midsummer festival of the Lord Sun (Inti) in December.

The early chroniclers were conquistadors and clerics. They were soon followed by the descendants of native Andean lords, making claims on the Spanish crown for services rendered, for the maintenance of pre-conquest privileges, and for the settlement of legal disputes with other native peoples. One such figure was Felipe Guamán Poma de Ayala, whose writings and drawings provide a rare glimpse into Inca life, albeit through the lens of colonial understanding.

Travelers' reports during the later Colonial Period also are important sources of information. Antonio Juan de Ulloa was part of a French expedition that voyaged to South America in the late 1730s, and during his sojourn he noted many practices of native peoples. Similarly, the great German geographer Alexander von Humboldt, who gave his name to the offshore Pacific current, published in 1811 a massive report on the biology and geology of the Andes, although he did not discuss Pre-Columbian ruins to any great extent.

ABOVE
In 1911, Hiram Bingham of Yale University was searching for Vilcabamba, the seat of Inca resistance against the Spanish, but stumbled upon Machu Picchu. Already known to locals, the great royal Inca estate was a revelation to the outside world.

The first serious report on Peruvian antiquities was made by Mariano Edward de Rivero, director of the National Museum, Lima, and his scientific colleague and friend, John James von Tschudi, in 1841. A version of their book was translated from Spanish into English. Perhaps a greater impact on the English-speaking world was made by William H. Prescott's *History of the Conquest of Peru*, a work of history rather than archaeology that excited much interest in the Andean past. Similarly, the lively style of Ephraim George Squier's *Peru: Incidents of Travel and Exploration in the Land of the Incas* (1877) made it a great success in drawing attention to the Andes.

One of the first archaeological investigations in the "Land of the Incas" was by Wilhelm Reiss and Alphons Stübel, who uncovered mummy bundles in a vast burial ground at Ancon, north of Lima, and published the results of their work in three large volumes between 1880 and 1887. Reiss and Stübel influenced their fellow German, Max Uhle, who helped them to publish notes and photographs taken at Tiwanaku. In the 1890s and 1900s Uhle went on to conduct pioneering research in Peru and Bolivia, and later worked in Chile and Ecuador. While Reiss and Stübel had mostly exposed graves, Uhle conducted true archaeology; he was one of the first to seize upon the importance of stratigraphic layers as the key to chronology. The basic chronology Uhle constructed for Peru remains valid to this day.

Following Uhle, other archaeologists began work in earnest in Peru, particularly Alfred Kroeber in the 1920s and 1930s. Of equal importance to Uhle as a founding father of Andean archaeology was Julio C. Tello, a highland Peruvian native who gained a Harvard degree and became Peru's leading archaeologist. Like Uhle, he laid foundations of scholarship that are still in many ways unmatched.

RIGHT
Among the many independent inventions of Andean people was the development of molds used in both metallurgy and, as in the example shown here, ceramics, for the mass production of goods.

The 1930s saw the flowering of Andean scholarship, including a great increase in native Bolivian, Peruvian, Chilean, and Ecuadorian researchers, and the support of many "non-vocational" scholars. Notable among the latter was Rafael Larco Hoyle, who laid the foundation for modern studies of Moche art and archaeology. From just prior to World War Two to the present day, Andean research has continued to grow to include scores of researchers and many different approaches to studying the past.

The sources for such studies are rich and plentiful. In the highlands, the remains of the past are impossible to miss: many Inca terraces, roads, and canals are still in use. On the coast, the dry deserts have preserved materials such as wood, fiber, bone, textiles, and wall paintings that in other environments would have long vanished, offering much to study, interpret, and ponder.

chapter 1

BEGINNINGS

FROM THE EARLIEST TIMES TO CA. 700BCE

LEFT

Decapitated heads, streaming blood, dismembered corpses, and entrails adorn the exterior stone wall of Cerro Sechín in the Casma valley. Whether celebrating a specific battle or generalized militarism, the grisly display underscores the sometimes turbulent times of ancient Peru (see also pages 32–33).

THE FIRST AMERICANS

PEOPLING THE CONTINENT

OPPOSITE
An Early Preceramic rock painting from Cuchimachay, east of Lima, depicting wild camelids, relatives of the llama and alpaca, of the *puna* (high plains) of highland Peru. Increasingly sophisticated hunting practices eventually led to the domestication of the llama and alpaca sometime between ca. 5200 and 4000BCE.

BELOW
The oldest South American artifacts are stone spearheads in the widespread "fluted fishtail" style, so called from its distinctive expanded stem. These examples, discovered in Fell's Cave in the far south of Chile, have been dated to ca. 9000–8000BCE.

The earliest Americans migrated to the New World toward the end of the last great ice age. For many years, archaeologists believed that they advanced from Asia across the Bering Land Bridge, which was exposed by lower sea levels. But it is now thought that people may also have arrived by water, picking their way along the Pacific coast; others may even have crossed the North Atlantic. Certainly, by around 10,000BCE humans were present throughout most of the Americas. The earliest human traces are large slender spearheads found at Clovis, New Mexico. Dated to 9500–9000BCE, the skillfully chipped stone points are both the first American technology and, because of their clear concern for aesthetics, the first American artworks.

Slightly later, distinctive spearheads also appeared in South America during the Early Preceramic (or Lithic) Period (ca. 10,000–3000BCE). Paleo-Indians, as the first Americans are called, used such spearheads to hunt mammoth, mastodon, and horse as well as the wild camelids—relatives of the llama and alpaca—of the *puna* (high plains) of Peru. Humans occupied highland Peru remarkably early, with sites such as Pikimachay, Pachamachay, and Telarmachay suggesting extensive camelid hunting. Paleo-Indians probably exploited local resources very quickly and diversified their ways of life just as rapidly, although scant remains can make interpretation difficult. For example, were the long, delicate spearheads of the Paiján "culture" (ca. 9000–8200BCE) of Peru's arid north coast used to spear fish? If so, it suggests Paiján people had adapted to a maritime economy. But the points are very brittle and could have acquired their concave shape through frequent resharpening. Unfortunately, the Paijan have left us little else to go on.

FISHERS AND FARMERS

At about the same time as the Paiján phenomenon, people began to exploit other coastal regions, at sites such as Amotape in northern Peru and Quebrada Tachay (the "Ring Site") and

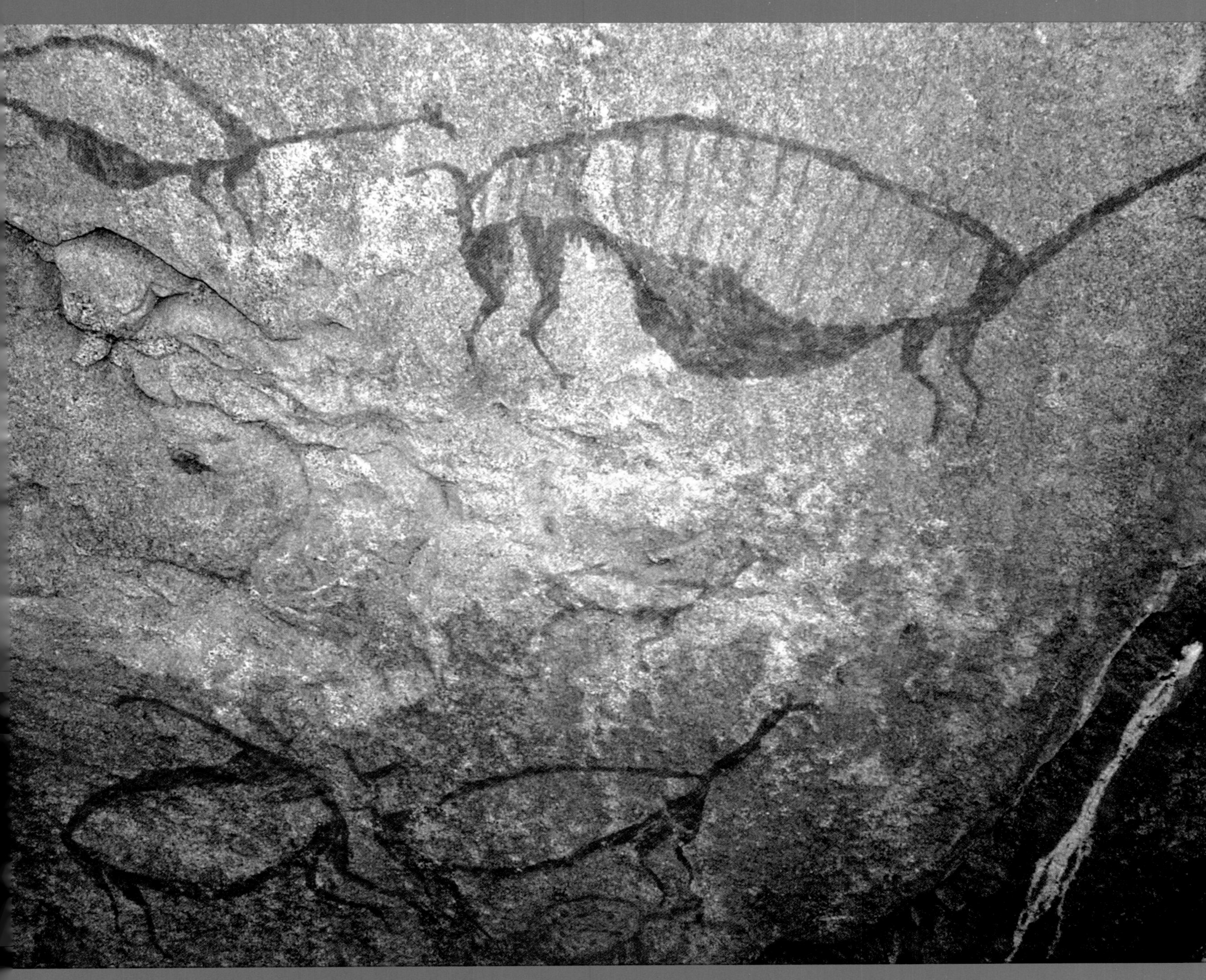

RIGHT
Among the oldest Andean works of art are two tiny carved gourds found at Huaca Prieta and dating to the Preceramic Period, ca. 3000–1800BCE. The carved stylized face on the gourd shown here resembles images from contemporary ceramics and other objects from Valdivia in Ecuador, where pottery was in use before Peru. The lid of the gourd bears a double-headed animal motif similar to others found on Huaca Prieta textiles and in Andean art down to the present. What the gourds contained is not known.

others on the south coast, dating from about 8600–7000BCE. Farther up the coast, people at the Las Vegas site in Ecuador exploited nearby mangrove swamps.

South of Lima, the site of Paloma on Peru's central coast was occupied many times between around 5000 and 3000BCE. People who stayed here—some for a few days at a time, others all year round—had three different sources of food and material: the hills, the sea, and the nearby Chilca River. For more than five millennia the dry climate has preserved reed huts as well as corpses wrapped in reed mats. The dead were buried with only a few offerings, such as a gourd bowl, a mussel shell filled with red pigment, or a bone awl pendant. However, other than a few beads and some cut shell disks, Palomans possessed little that could be considered art.

Many similar places with multiple resource zones soon came to be settled all year round, or almost so. Communities in the middle and upper Zaña valley, for instance, featured the beginnings of open public spaces, indicating a more settled lifestyle. Living in one place allowed people to accumulate more goods, and artifacts expressing ideas about the world begin to appear between about 3500 and 2500BCE.

THE TWIN-HEADED SERPENT: HUACA PRIETA

In 1946 Junius B. Bird excavated Huaca Prieta ("Dark Sacred Mound") at the mouth of the Chicama River on Peru's north coast. A large site first occupied during the

Preceramic Period (ca. 3000–1800BCE), Huaca Prieta got its name from the cinders of countless fires among the domestic debris which, over centuries of occupation, had formed a great oval mound some 420ft (125m) long and 40ft (12m) high.

Bird found remarkable evidence of the ancient lives of the fisherfolk and farmers of the mound, such as subterranean houses to shelter from the chilly winds; plant and animal remains; and fishing equipment—including a large cotton net with gourd floats. He also found more than six thousand pieces and fragments of cloth, together with countless scraps. After careful cleaning, these rags turned out to have been not woven but made with a sophisticated twining technique to produce decorative patterns. Some threads had originally been dyed so that the patterns were visible. Over the centuries the dyes had faded, and it was only through great diligence that the earliest corpus of Andean art was brought to light.

The designs in the Huaca Prieta textiles are sophisticated and highly geometric, mostly abstract renditions of creatures of the sea and shore such as crabs, fish, snakes, and birds, as well as stylized human-like figures. Some motifs, such as a two-headed snake in an "S" pattern, have continued to be used in Andean art down to the present day. One of the most striking images is that of a condor, wings spread, with a snake in its belly. The image may be linked with a myth, perhaps similar to the much later story of the eagle and snake as a sign for the founding of the Aztec capital.

In a grave at Huaca Prieta, Bird also found two small fragile carved gourds. They are of great interest because their style of decoration resembles that of early Valdivia pottery in contemporary Ecuador. People in Peru did not yet make pottery at this time, but they apparently were in contact, perhaps indirectly, with people who did. This suggests an active movement of people over considerable distances. Indeed, by about 2500BCE cultures in Peru began to increase the pace of change considerably.

ABOVE
A ceramic plaque from Valdivia bearing an incised stylized face similar to that on the gourd on page 24—possible evidence of long-distance contacts.

THE TEMPLE OF THE FANGS

In striking contrast to the plainly painted Preceramic Period sites (see pages 28–30) which preceded them, some Initial Period ceremonial and sacred complexes are elaborately decorated with images of monsters and other beings that appear to represent the emergence of a complex religious symbolism. At Cardal in the Lurín River valley near Lima, Richard Burger found a colored adobe frieze of a huge stylized mouth with great fangs, surrounding the central atrium and stairs of the complex. Those entering the small building up the stairs would therefore be symbolically "eaten" by a deity. Also on the upper platform was a structure that contained a small stepped altar designed like a miniature terraced temple and very likely also symbolizing a mountain. In fact, the temple as a whole was probably considered a symbolic mountain. Thus the altar-mountain, temple-mountain, and the "real" mountains of the distant Andes were linked in a replicating pattern from micro to macro scales. The central temple may have been the site of rituals conducted by priests. However, at least one arm of the U-shaped complex contained several sunken circular plazas that may have been where separate groups performed their own ceremonies, similar to the separate chambers of the Kotosh religious tradition (see pages 28–29). As at Kotosh, these may have been individual extended families or other groups from rural areas.

At Moxeke on the north coast of Peru, huge colorfully painted molded adobe heads and upper torsos, each distinctively different, were placed facing out of the exterior wall of a temple complex. Perhaps each was the titular deity of a clan or other group. At another Initial Period temple complex, Garagay in the Chillón River valley, the atrium frieze consists of brightly painted monsters (see illustrations, opposite). They are usually separated by an abstract motif resembling a wave or stylized feather. The motif includes a simple step-like design that echoes the "mountain-altar" found at Cardal. This motif suggests that in addition to representational depictions of monsters and other creatures, a form of abstract symbolism was beginning to develop at some sites, perhaps representing the religious center or its cult.

RIGHT, ABOVE AND BELOW
Two details of polychrome adobe friezes of fanged monster heads from the atrium of the temple of Garagay. We do not know the myths that lie behind these images but they are likely to have already been very old when the friezes were made. The artists did not present the images in a narrative form but as isolated motifs and figures, such as the disembodied head encircled by a band. This suggests that the mythic narratives of which these distinctive figures formed a part would have been familiar to those who saw them.

CEREMONIAL CENTERS

PLACES OF SACRED RITUAL

The large ceremonial sites of ancient Peru evolved out of the creation of initially small ritual spaces. The earliest such ritual centers used two basic elements that continued in use through Inca times: the plaza (open area or court) and the platform (raised area). Later Preceramic people favored sunken plazas, often circular with maybe one or more platforms. One early form was a small sunken plaza, or patio, perhaps where people of one clan performed rituals within a shared sacred area. This pattern was first noted at Kotosh in Peru's central highlands, where archaeologists found many square adobe-and-stone chambers that had been built, later filled in, then built over. Painted on the stairway to one chamber was a stylized snake, while the chamber entrance was red, a color used for temples through Inca times. Inside, the

RIGHT
The so-called Temple of the Crossed Hands, one of many ritual chamber at Kotosh. The niches with the two crossed-hand friezes flank the entrance, center. The chamber, just under 33ft (10m) square and 6.5ft (2m) high, once had a flat roof of wooden beams covered with clay. Such rooms were key components of a widespread Initial Period cult in which small groups gathered in darkened chambers, probably to commune with ancestors.

entrance was flanked by niches, another essential element of Andean architecture through late prehistory. Below each niche is a pair of crossed arms and hands of mud plaster, the earliest example of an Andean frieze. In the niches archaeologists discovered the remains of camelids and guinea pigs, as well as two human-like figurines of unbaked clay. These suggest that the chambers may have been used for fertility rites, probably conducted by local clan leaders and their families. The environment was evidently one in which everyone had relatively equal status—like many of the Kotosh chambers this one had a low adobe bench running around the interior wall and a small firepit in the middle.

There are many sites similar to Kotosh, and Richard Burger called the chambers and the practices inferred from them the Kotosh religious tradition. One of the best-preserved and most elaborate sites is La Galgada in the valley of the Tablachaca, a tributary of the Santa River. The dry climate preserved many perishable items in old ceremonial rooms used as crypts. As well as the fine textiles in which the dead were wrapped, there were large bone pins inlaid with a blue-green turquoise-like stone, and large necklaces of distinctive double-holed red stone beads. The colors may have had sacred significance—perhaps blue-green for life-giving water, red for earth and blood.

ABOVE
Valdivia stone and clay figurines dating to ca. 2000BCE. Almost always female, such figures were probably created for a variety of purposes, including as fertility charms. The elaborate coiffures are typical, while the arms held around the stomach may be a dancing posture—one still seen today among tropical forest women. The Valdivia culture is named for a coastal site in Ecuador north of the Gulf of Guayaquil (see also illustration on page 25).

BUILDING TO IMPRESS

In the Preceramic Period stacked platforms, each slightly larger than the one above, became widely popular. It required no complex engineering to build high, ziggurat-like structures that would impress crowds gathered to watch priests or officials act out their roles above. By the later Preceramic Period complexes of enclosed spaces were

BELOW
Figurines continue in later periods but they are commonest in the earliest eras of Andean prehistory. Usually depicting females, clay models such as this one may have been used in women's fertility rites. They are often found broken and such damage may have been part of the rituals.

also fairly numerous, but plazas and raised mass remained popular. The building of large complexes of stone and adobe increased dramatically after around 2500BCE. Some of the earliest are at Aspero and Caral, in the Supe valley on the north central coast. It is unclear whether these ritual sites were built by ruling élites or by several communities coming together. Societies were perhaps becoming more stratified at this time, but to what extent is uncertain.

The early large ceremonial centers are on the stretch of Peruvian coast where seafood was most abundant, and there are similar highland sites on the same latitudes. However, an increasing range of agricultural produce also appears to have contributed to the surplus of resources and labor required to support such huge centers. Covering scores of hectares, they owed their size and success more to the organization of labor than the complexity of their building technology.

In the following Initial Period (ca. 1800–700BCE), people in Peru took up true weaving and ceramics (fired pottery). In spite of their size, the Preceramic complexes bear little evidence of decoration except for uniform coats of paint. However, Initial Period ceremonial centers began to bear increasingly elaborate designs, including striking depictions of monsters and other beings, as well as more abstract motifs (see pages 26–27). Perhaps ancient Andean peoples developed ceramic and weaving techniques not because they necessarily offered better ways to make containers or cloth, but because both media could display symbolic decoration more effectively.

Many of the great Preceramic and Initial Period sacred complexes followed the U-shaped structure, with one arm slightly longer than the other. This may have expressed concepts better known for later Andean prehistory, in which societies were divided into two slightly unequal but mutually dependent sectors, often expressed as "upper" and "lower" communities.

ABOVE

Uyucua (bone figurines) from Cerro Narrío in the southern Ecuadorian highlands, center of another early Andean culture. These anthropomorphic figures are enigmatic but sport a distinctive headdress or hat—headgear was of great importance to later Andean peoples.

COMPETING FESTIVALS

The broad similarity of these temple complexes was probably due to widespread shared ancient Andean ideas of the cosmos and the beings that dwelt in it. At such centers people from the surrounding countryside would attend "religious" events that were probably an exciting mix of what we would consider entertainment, feasting, and religion. Huge sculptures, bright colors, and elaborate and dramatic rituals were designed to thrill and excite great crowds gathered in large plazas to witness spectacles at the top of the temples. Perhaps they assembled first in their own communal temples to imbibe drinks such as the alcoholic *chicha* or the hallucinogenic San Pedro cactus, before entering the central plazas for events that would bind them, temporarily

LEFT
The stark images at Cerro Sechín include this warrior in helmet, face paint, and girdle, wielding a mace or spear-thrower. He may be clutching a wound, from which flows stylized blood. Strife, it seems, may have beset the last decades or even centuries of the Initial Period.

at least, into one community. At Mina Perdida, near Cardal, Richard and Lucy Burger found a puppet-like painted gourd figure with moveable arms and legs, probably one of many enchantments for the temple crowds.

The sheer size of these sites suggests that their construction required a huge amount of labor. For many years it seems that when they were not engaged in everyday survival, people in Peru were chiefly involved in constructing such massive complexes. Nevertheless, many temples appear to have been built, remodeled, then rapidly abandoned. In the lower Lurín River valley there are at least three Initial Period complexes with overlapping dates of occupation. It has been suggested that these temples were built competitively, each vying to attract followers among the same rural folk, much as competing amusement parks struggle for visitors in southern Florida today.

BELOW
Cerro Sechín images such as this severed head may be linked to sacrifices, but if so such rites do not appear to have reflected any higher purpose, such as feeding the rhythms of the cosmos, as was the case in later cultures.

WAR AND SACRIFICE

Some centers may have had a darker purpose than shared communal ceremonies. Near the vast north coast complex of Sechín Alto, the outer wall of the temple known as Cerro Sechín is engraved with severed human heads and limbs and other large gruesome images. Such images are more likely to portray the grisly trophies of war than to celebrate regional community solidarity. The images suggest that late in the Initial Period, times were unsettled, although actual warfare may have been relatively infrequent. Cerro Sechín is unique in its portrayal of slaughtered humans and only more research will uncover the reasons why Initial Period societies underwent dramatic changes. These changes are indicated by the rise of a powerful religious cult that spread far and wide across ancient Peru from its highland center, which is known today as Chavín de Huantar.

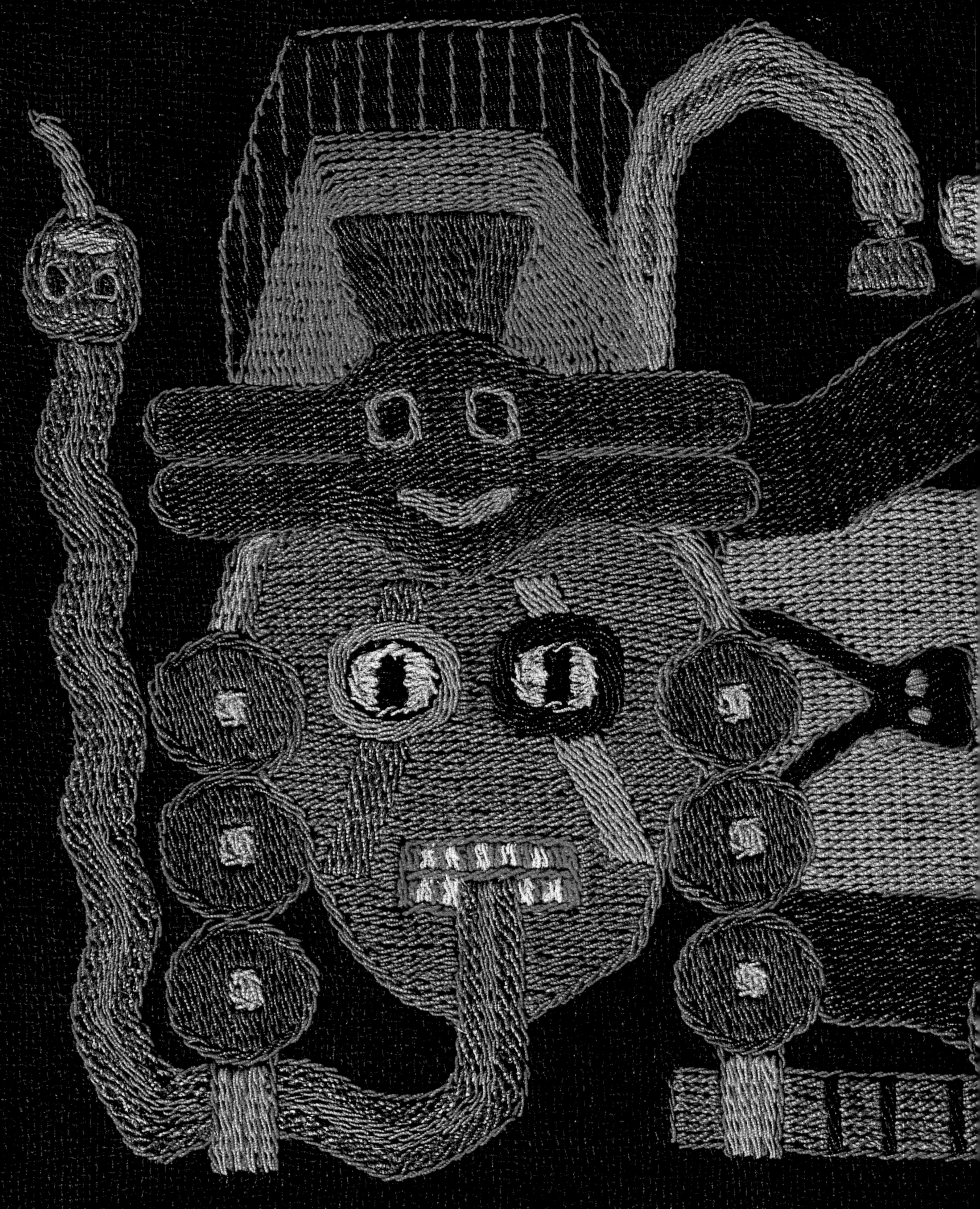

chapter 2

MONSTER GODS OF THE COSMOS

THE EARLY HORIZON

CA. 700BCE–CA. 0CE

LEFT

Embroidered on a mantle of the Paracas culture is a "bird shaman" or spirit impersonator with outstretched cape and claws. The nasal emanations are similar to snuff mucus on contemporary Chavín sculpture, as are the snake-head appendages, outstretched arms, and frontal posture.

THE PILGRIM'S JOURNEY

THE MYSTERIES OF CHAVÍN

BELOW
The snow-capped, western Cordillera Blanca of the Andes runs parallel to the barren Cordillera Negra, together forming a large intermontane valley, the Callejon de Huaylas, which facilitated north–south communication in ancient Peru. Chavín de Huantar lay just to the west of this often bitterly cold area.

He had reached the threshold of the climax of his journey. The priest from the far north coast wrapped his best cloak tighter around him against the unfamiliar chill of the highlands. Waiting for those who would lead him to the ultimate mysteries in the temple of Chavín de Huantar, he thought back on his long journey. He and his small retinue had traveled for many days, first across the perilous deserts of the coast and then, finally, up the Santa River, along the broad valley with the dark mountains on the right and the snow-capped peaks on the left. After more days of travel they had finally turned in the direction of the rising sun, through a high pass where the icy cold bit into their flesh, and then down to the high valley that was the home of the Great God.

Upon arrival they had been lodged in a place outside of the temple precincts. There, the pilgrim priest met many others who had journeyed from other lands. Some

BELOW
A carved projection, or tenon, from the exterior wall of the complex at Chavín de Huantar—the only tenon still in situ more than two millennia after it was first set in place.

from far to the south told how they had abandoned their old gods after strangers had appeared with a new message and fantastic images, painted on textiles, of the Great God, his incarnations, and the other deities of his heavenly realm.

Now, the priest had been summoned to enter, alone, into the presence of the God. His assistants accompanied him into the great plaza, in front of the magnificent stone temple that rose high against the backdrop of the mountains to the west. They had brought with them the most precious offerings of their realm—spondylus and strombus (conch) shells and examples of their finest pottery—but could go no further than the entrance to the temple. Amid chanting, drumbeats, and the deep throbbing of golden trumpets, by the flickering light of torches they handed their offerings to the officials who came to greet them.

Surrounded by the temple priests, the pilgrim from the north coast was led into the house of the god. They walked through a labyrinth of tunnels, twisting and turning through darkness lit by torches in the wall. Small rooms to the side occasionally revealed a figure in a trance, eyes staring ahead. They reached a chamber with more small rooms to each side. Here the priests told him to empty the contents of the beautiful pots he held into golden bowls that they held out to him. Then, they told him simply to discard the fine vessels by hurling them into another side chamber. The pilgrim hesitated—he had guarded these personal offerings so long on the hard journey—but their eyes told him he must obey.

A VISION OF MONSTERS

The pilgrim was led to another room, where a temple priest used a small stone mortar, in the shape of a fantastic jaguar, to grind some dried seeds into a fine powder. The pilgrim had fasted for many days and now his weakness and the experiences in the labyrinth were beginning to affect his mind. One by one, the priests inhaled the powder, placed on a beautifully carved palette, through a short tube. Now it was his turn.

The powder seared his nose, which began to stream with mucus. He looked around the room and saw that all the temple priests had runny noses too. Then, as the narcotic powder began to affect his mind, he saw their faces changing, eyes bulging and mouths drawing back to reveal teeth turning into fangs. The priests were becoming fierce animals and monsters and then he realized that he too was no longer human.

The party moved on through the labyrinth again. Colorful designs danced before the pilgrim's eyes and part of him knew that he had entered the world of the gods, indeed that he himself had become a god. He turned a corner and saw, at the intersection of labyrinth tunnels, the Great God itself, towering high above him. He prostrated himself before the image—was it grinning or snarling, or both?—and then the god spoke. Its voice seemed to boom through eternity. It told the pilgrim from the north many things about the deepest secrets of life, answering his questions without him having to ask them. The god also told him to build a temple for its worship, before the pilgrim seemed to fall into a swirling hole of color with darkness at its center.

It was dawn when the pilgrim came to his senses. He was back among his companions, but he had been transformed by his experience. After a few more ceremonies outside of the temple, the group began their long journey home.

OPPOSITE
It is likely that only the most honored pilgrims to Chavín were allowed onto the upper terrace of the temple and to pass through the Black and White Portal (center, opposite) into the New Temple. Such great care was taken in the construction of the portal that even the interior fill stones of the structure were carefully laid in place although it was never to be seen. The fill may be seen here in the area above and to either side of the portal, where the finer stone cladding has been stripped away.

THE GROWTH OF CHAVÍN

Only a few details of the story of the pilgrim's journey to Chavín de Huantar, around two and a half thousand years ago, are conjectural. Although these are imagined events, they are based on a careful evaluation of architectural, archaeological, and art historical evidence. The temple complex is located high in a valley that drains, eventually, to the Amazon River. The temple stands also at a pass that leads westward across the mountains to the Santa River valley, which runs northwards and then into the Pacific. Chavín was therefore in an ideal position to receive pilgrims and other visitors, as well as goods, from all three of the major environmental zones of the Andes.

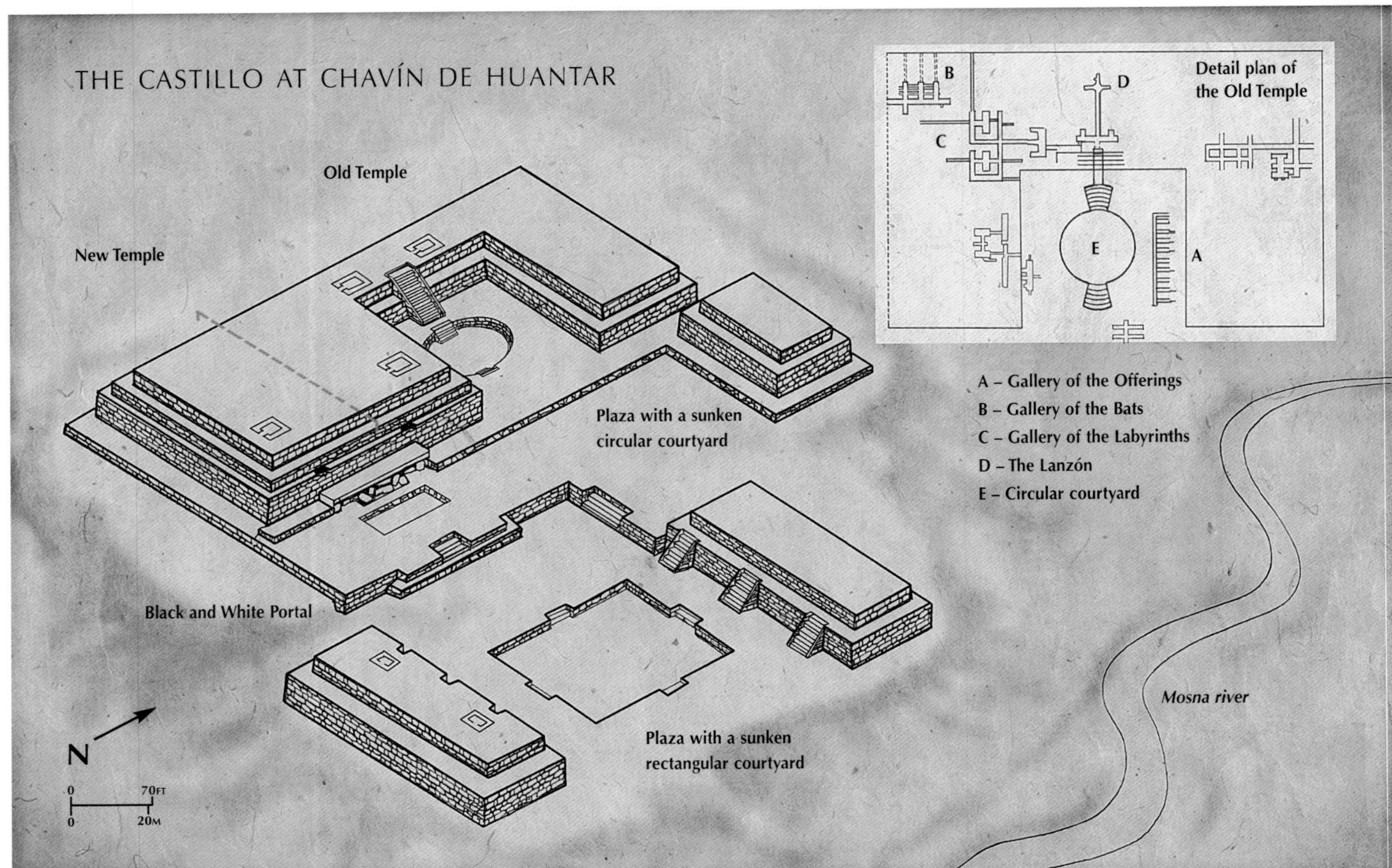

ABOVE
The Chavín temple grew through time as pilgrims brought wealth to the site. To the Old Temple (right), was added the New Temple, built at the height of the site's power (ca. 400—200BCE). Near and within the the Old Temple complex are a series of galleries, including the Gallery of the Offerings (A), the Gallery of the Bats (B), and the Gallery of the Labyrinths (C). The Lanzón (D) is located centrally. The famous Black and White Portal fronts the New Temple, while the Old Temple is fronted by a sunken circular courtyard (E) in its plaza.

The temple grew through time, starting with a small U-shaped structure known as the "Old Temple," built some time between 1000 and 500BCE. The south section was subsequently expanded to create the "New Temple" (ca. 500–400BCE). The entire complex is known today as the Castillo ("the Castle"), a misnomer given to the site by the Spanish. The following two centuries saw both the zenith of Chavín and its final phase (ca. 400–200BCE).

A large plaza in front of the Castillo could have held several hundred people with ease. But only a few at a time could have entered the labyrinth of narrow passageways inside the structure, guided by those familiar with its twists and turns. Side chambers in this maze were found to hold jars of food, probably offerings to support temple priests. In another set of small chambers, known as the Gallery of the Offerings, broken but finely made pottery vessels were found, with different styles in each chamber. This appears to have been a place to which pilgrims came from throughout ancient Peru and where, at some point in the ritual proceedings, they smashed the bottles and bowls containing the offerings they had brought. What these fine vessels

had in them is unknown, but we might suspect that they were precious things that were representative of the bearers' places of origin.

ABOVE
This feline worked in sheet gold has a characteristic Chavín tail that transforms into a snake with cat ears. Two profile heads merge to form a front-facing fanged face on the animal's back. Three holes in the rear offer evidence that it was originally sewn to a textile. Other minor details suggest that this Chavín-style piece may have been made on the north coast of what is now Peru.

THE FACE OF THE MONSTER

The imagined narcotic-induced experience of the pilgrim is also rooted in sound archaeology. At the University of Pennsylvania Museum there is a stone mortar in the shape of a stylized jaguar, with the grinding surface on its back. This is only one of many examples of mortars found in the ancient Andes—palettes for inhaling snuff are known for Preceramic sites, so the tradition was already ancient by the time of Chavín. Jaguars are jungle animals, and the assorted jungle motifs were associated with shamanism and powerful mind-altering plants. To this day the pods and seeds of various members of the pea family are an important source of a number of traditional hallucinogens in Peru, Bolivia, and other parts of South America. In ancient times, stimulants appear to have been used only for ritual purposes.

There is other evidence for supposing that the inhalation of hallucinogens formed part of the experience of some of the priests and, possibly, special visitors to the temple complex. Around the exterior of the main temple at Chavín there were a series of large stone heads with projections, or tenons, at the back so that they could

BELOW
The distinct north coast style of Tembladera was part of the Chavín world. The ear ornaments of this ceramic flute player are also found on the Lanzón at Chavín, but his facial markings and loincloth mean he is not from the central highlands. Throughout the Andes, music was used to summon divinities.

RIGHT
Said to have been found with the effigy spoon on page 45, this gold gorget is in classic Chavín de Huantar style. The interlace border and front-facing head are secondary design elements in the Chavín stone-carving repertoire that here have been given primary place.

be inserted into the wall (see illustrations, pages 37 and 46). Almost all these tenon heads have fallen and are now kept inside the Castillo. The sculptures can be arranged in a sequence, beginning with rather benign human-like visages and gradually metamorphosing into the faces of monsters.

Prominent features in this change from human to supernatural are increasingly bulging eyes and, most importantly, bands apparently descending from the nostrils of the sculptures. These bands have been interpreted as a sign of the effects of inhaled drugs. When snorted through the nostrils, psychotropic substances stimulate the production of mucus, and runny noses occur at the same time as hallucinations (see illustration, page 34).

THE GREAT GOD OF CHAVÍN

Many gods may have been worshipped at Chavín de Huantar, where there are depictions of a number of different deities. But deep in the temple complex, inside the Old Temple, stands the cult image known as the Lanzón. The word is Spanish and means "big lance," because the sculpture looks like a huge spearhead, jabbed into the ground. It is 15ft (4.5m) high and roughly trapezoidal in cross-section. It has stood in the same place since at least around 700BCE, if not a century or two earlier, at the intersection of two of the labyrinth's tunnels.

The Lanzón depicts what the archaeologist Richard Burger has called the "Supreme Deity" of Chavín, the unnamed "Great God" of the imaginary pilgrim. It has a human body and a monster head with fangs. Its pupils are set high in their eye orbits, a common Chavín motif signifying a trance state. One arm is raised upward and one points down. The god sports long fingernails, dangling ear ornaments, and an elaborate belt over a fringed tunic.

LEFT
The Lanzón, deep inside the New Temple of Chavín (see diagram, page 40), stands on the central axis of the Old Temple and at the crossroads in a labyrinth of tunnels. The shaft above its head has earned it the name of "Big Lance," from its resemblance to a blade thrust into the earth. This form is also found centuries later in non-representational Inca sculpture.

When the chamber of the Great God was explored in the 1930s, a member of the team wandered away and found himself in a small room above the Lanzón. A slit in the rocks allowed him to see his companions below, around the statue. When he called out to them his voice boomed dramatically in the chamber below. The incident strongly suggests that the Great God served as an oracle. Oracles were well known at the time of the Spanish arrival, and the tradition was evidently a very old one (see pages 128–131). In the case of Chavín, the statue itself may have been thought to speak, since the priest who served as the god's voice would have been hidden from view.

The small space in which the Lanzón stands and the hidden oracle chamber together suggest that only one or two seekers of knowledge at a time would have been admitted into the Great God's presence. Administering psychotropic drugs to pilgrims would have intensified their confrontation with the supernatural.

Finally, the oracle's instruction to the pilgrim to build a temple to the Great God in his own land is also based on sound evidence. The foreign ceramics in the Gallery of the Offerings indicate that some pilgrims traveled to Chavín from very far away, and Chavín cult centers were indeed established elsewhere in Peru. This suggests that one of the messages of the gods of Chavín de Huantar was to spread their cult far and wide.

RIGHT
This Chavín spoon was made with great technical skill from 22 separate gold and silver pieces and it is one of the earliest 3-dimensional sheet metal sculptures in the Andes. The figure blows a conch shell (of silver) to summon the gods, and contains pellets that would have enabled the spoon to serve as a rattle. The object may have been used in rituals employing hallucinogenic snuff.

UNITY FROM DIVERSITY: THE ART OF CHAVÍN

Chavín art is commonly considered the first great art style of ancient Peru. In a sense this is not true, for fine artworks were made in the preceding Initial Period (see Chapter 1). But this art was expressed in local, variable, styles, with an underlying unity in commonly shared ideas. Chavín took those common ideas, as well as some general artistic styles, and reinterpreted them, adding its own flair. The result was art that shared features of what had gone before but was also something completely new.

Some scholars have proposed that Chavín was essentially a religious cult that spread its message through missionaries, who convinced local people to join the highland sect. It has been suggested that large textiles painted with Chavín designs, discovered at Karwa on the south coast of Peru, were used by Chavín missionaries as easily portable instruments in the conversion process.They might have been hung up to create instant shrines, or used perhaps as teaching aids to instruct converts on the form and nature of the new gods. This proposal has received much attention, but it is difficult to prove. Some textiles from Karwa were very large, made of 3ft (1m)-wide strips of cloth sewn together, and therefore hard to hang, suggesting that they might have been something more like carpets. Perhaps they served as "stages" on which to perform rituals. Furthermore, some of the textiles appear to show a Chavín-like deity but with cotton plants springing from it. Cotton is not a highland product, so a classic highland depiction was adapted to local concerns and expressions.

THE CAYMAN OF THE COSMOS

The unique aspect of the creative genius of Chavín artists was their synthesis of tropical forest, highland, and coastal symbolism. One of the most powerful examples of this mixing is the Tello Obelisk, named for the Peruvian archaeologist Julio C. Tello who conducted major research at the site in the 1930s. Like the Lanzón, it is a notched shaft of granite about 8ft (2.52m) high and 1ft (0.32m) wide, with four flat sides. It is

LEFT
Once found adorning the exterior of Chavín's New Temple, tenon heads such as this one showed the stages of transformation from a human to a supernatural being (see also page 37). The blank stare of this human head expresses an early stage in a drug-induced trance, signaled by the mucus only just beginning to flow from the nostrils.

BELOW
One of the most spectacular sculptures at Chavín is the Tello Obelisk, which depicts an anthropomorphic cayman as the progenitor of useful plants and animals. At the notch near its top is a stepped cross with a circle in its center, a motif symbolizing the unity of the cosmos. Widespread in the Pre-Columbian Andes, the motif is found in Andean art to this day.

carved all over with the features of a hybrid monster sprouting plants and various creatures. The monster's chief features are those of the black cayman, a crocodile-like reptile of the tropical forest that grows up to 20ft (6m) in length. This cosmic cayman stands vertically, perhaps in flight, for it sports the tail feathers of a hawk or eagle, thus combining the features of a master of the air with those of the king of the waters.

Each side bears images of domesticated plants. Those of the left side cayman ("cayman A"), including manioc and peanuts, grow below ground while those of the right side cayman ("cayman B"), including chilli pepper and bottle gourd, grow above. Donald Lathrap suggested that cayman A was the Cayman of the Underworld and B the Cayman of the Sky. Whether it depicts one cayman or two, the sculpture unites a host of opposites, such as the rainy season and the dry, animals and plants, above and below. A stepped cross motif, symbolizing cosmic unity, also appears on the Lanzón and may be a mark of the highest Chavín gods. In its high mountain sanctuary, the Tello Obelisk combined tropical forest and coastal symbolism, as did the temple and the cult themselves—thus proclaiming Chavín de Huantar as the center of the cosmos.

THE GOD OF THE TWO STAFFS

The Lanzón and the Tello Obelisk likely depict the two most important Chavín deities. The Raimondi Stela or Stone is a carved slab that may also represent the Supreme Deity and is noteworthy for its dazzling display of Chavín artistic magic. The god faces the viewer and sports a huge rayed headdress. When seen upside down, the headdress turns into stacked monster faces beneath the visage of the god, now smiling rather than frowning. Unless they were held by their feet, ancient observers would not have seen this, but perhaps it registered in the drugged state, intensifying the awe of the viewer.

The upright image of the god, holding a staff in each hand and usually with bent legs, was already centuries old by the time it appeared at Chavín. With variations, usually in what the deity holds, this image continued in use throughout Andean

BELOW
One of a pair said to be from Chongoyape, on the north coast, this gold sheet metal plaque may have been part of an ear ornament or was sewn onto cloth. It depicts the prime deity of Chavín as represented on the Lanzón (page 44) and the Raimondi Stela (opposite). The main elements of the god receive attention here, such as his large head and frontal position.

RIGHT
This detail of the Raimondi Stela shows Chavín stone sculpture at its finest. The polished, flat surface, crisply carved lines, and deep spaces were made in hard granite without metal tools. Known as the Staff God, this is a variant of the principal Chavín deity. Its headdress turns into a monster head when inverted.

prehistory. This Staff God may have represented different concepts throughout its long use but it was likely an authoritative deity who presided over others, perhaps over the cosmos itself. A staff is an important sign of authority among traditional peoples today, so it is likely that a god holding one was also of very high rank and charged with both overseeing and protecting those in his charge.

Yet another representation of the Supreme Deity of Chavín appears in a stone panel that may have once adorned the outside of the New Temple, a large structure that was added to the Old Temple. This time, the god has Medusa-like snake hair and holds a strombus (conch) shell in his right hand and a spondylus in his left, representing male and female principles respectively. Other panels show a butterfly or bat, a viscacha (a large burrowing rodent), and other creatures.

The roles of these animals in the pantheon of Chavín gods are hard to determine. In front of the Old Temple a circular sunken plaza was adorned with a procession of deities with a parallel parade of jaguars underneath them. Elsewhere, sculpture fragments depict deities or men with knives and trophy heads, while another large sculpture shows the head of a bird of prey. A long carving of a supernatural being with cayman features adorned an entry to the large rectangular plaza facing the New Temple—but it is uncertain whether this is the same cayman-deity as that depicted on the Lanzón.

GUARDIANS OF THE TEMPLE

The cult of Chavín and its gods must have evolved over the hundreds of years that the temple was in use. Jaguars and eagles appear to have served as minor Chavín deities throughout that time—these creatures

LEFT
In this detail of a carving from Chavín de Huantar, the tongue of the front-faced monster can be read as a series of partial profile faces, the last of which sports a fanged mouth (which itself is the left side of another front-facing creature). Such visual effects are hallmarks of Chavín style, as is the bilateral symmetry.

RIGHT
The dry north coast of Peru preserved normally perishable items such as this bone spatula, which is delicately carved in Chavín style with a variety of feline, bird, and anthropomorphic motifs. The spatula, which retains traces of red pigment, was probably used for hallucinogenic snuff, like the gold and silver spoon shown earlier (see page 45).

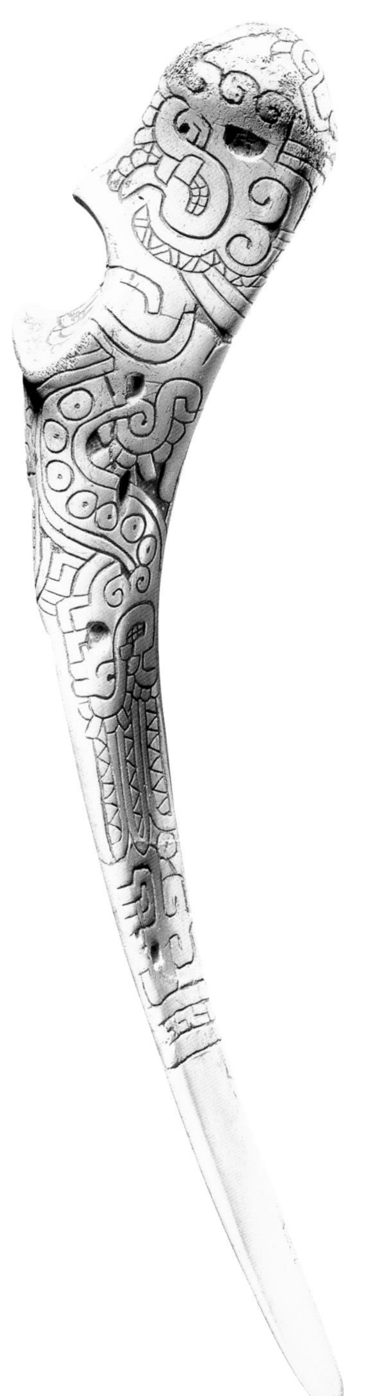

parade not only around the sunken plaza of the Old Temple but also across the front of the New Temple. Above the main entrance to the New Temple, a series of hybrid creatures with a combination of bird and feline features marched toward one another.

Another display of Chavín, and Andean, dualism appears in the use of black limestone and white granite in the temple's entrance portal. This dualism is repeated in the carvings on the portal's two great stone columns: on one an anthropomorphized female crested eagle has attributes relating to water; on the other is a similar, male, figure accompanied by celestial symbolism. These bird-gods were the guardians of the entrance to what was, in its day, the holiest shrine in the Andes. But there came a time when the highland temple of Chavín de Huantar was abandoned and pilgrims no longer stopped there—except, perhaps, to make a small offering to an ancient cult whose power was remembered long after the names of its deities were forgotten.

AFTER THE FALL

It is not known whether the cultural unity that Chavín had provided for eight centuries unraveled slowly or underwent a rapid collapse. One or more climatic disasters, such as a catastrophic El Niño that brought devastating rain to the coast and drought to the highlands, may have played a part. But vigorous religions can survive natural calamities or, at least, reformulate themselves. For the Chavín religion to have ceased to exist entirely there must also have been social and cultural stresses, and environmental disasters were perhaps the final blow to hope and faith.

Whatever the causes, instability followed Chavín's collapse. At Chavín itself, carpets of broken pottery shards littering the ground in front of once sacred buildings evoke images of the barbarians camping in the Forum at Rome. Elsewhere, valley communities moved for security up into the high hills. Their new settlements were crudely built and often ringed with defensive walls; mollusk shells and fishbones attest to trips to the beach and the hauling of food up steep inclines to safety.

COLORS OF ETERNITY

THE GLORIES OF PARACAS

OPPOSITE
This spectacular shell and bluestone pectoral is in a style that was popular for centuries in ancient Peru. However, the small profile feline heads indicate that it may well be of the Chavín era, contemporary with Paracas. The reused drilled beads may once have been part of a necklace and may have added value to the collar owing to their antiquity or the status of the former owner.

After the murky dark age following Chavín's demise, new cultural forms arose with distinct regional flavors. The people of the south coast of Peru may have received Chavín missionaries or they may have simply participated in a generalized Chavín-like cult. Whichever the case, they developed early on a distinct ceramic tradition that was one of the most colorful of the ancient Andes. Chavín pottery was masterful in its use of carefully handcrafted ceramics, frequently featuring elaborately modeled figures or exquisitely incised and often highly intricate designs, much like their stone carving. Chavín ceramicists had delighted mostly in dark brown and black ceramics that employed textured surfaces, mirror-like polishes, or a combination of both on the same vessel. But the people of the south coast took an entirely different approach to their pottery.

CREATING IN CLAY: THE ART OF THE POTTER

From around 800 until 100BCE—and therefore largely contemporary with the Chavín culture—the Paracas ceramic style was popular between the Chincha and Acarí valleys in southern Peru. The style takes its name from the remote Paracas peninsula, about 150 miles (240km) south of Lima. Like all New World ceramics, those of Paracas were not made with a potter's wheel. Vessels were made by making "coils" (rings) of clay and building them up, joining and smoothing one coil on top of the other. Elsewhere a second non-wheel method was that of the "paddle and anvil" technique. This method usually involved partly forming the base of a vessel, often by molding clay over another pot or some other form, and then adding clay to it and gently patting it to join the other clay and

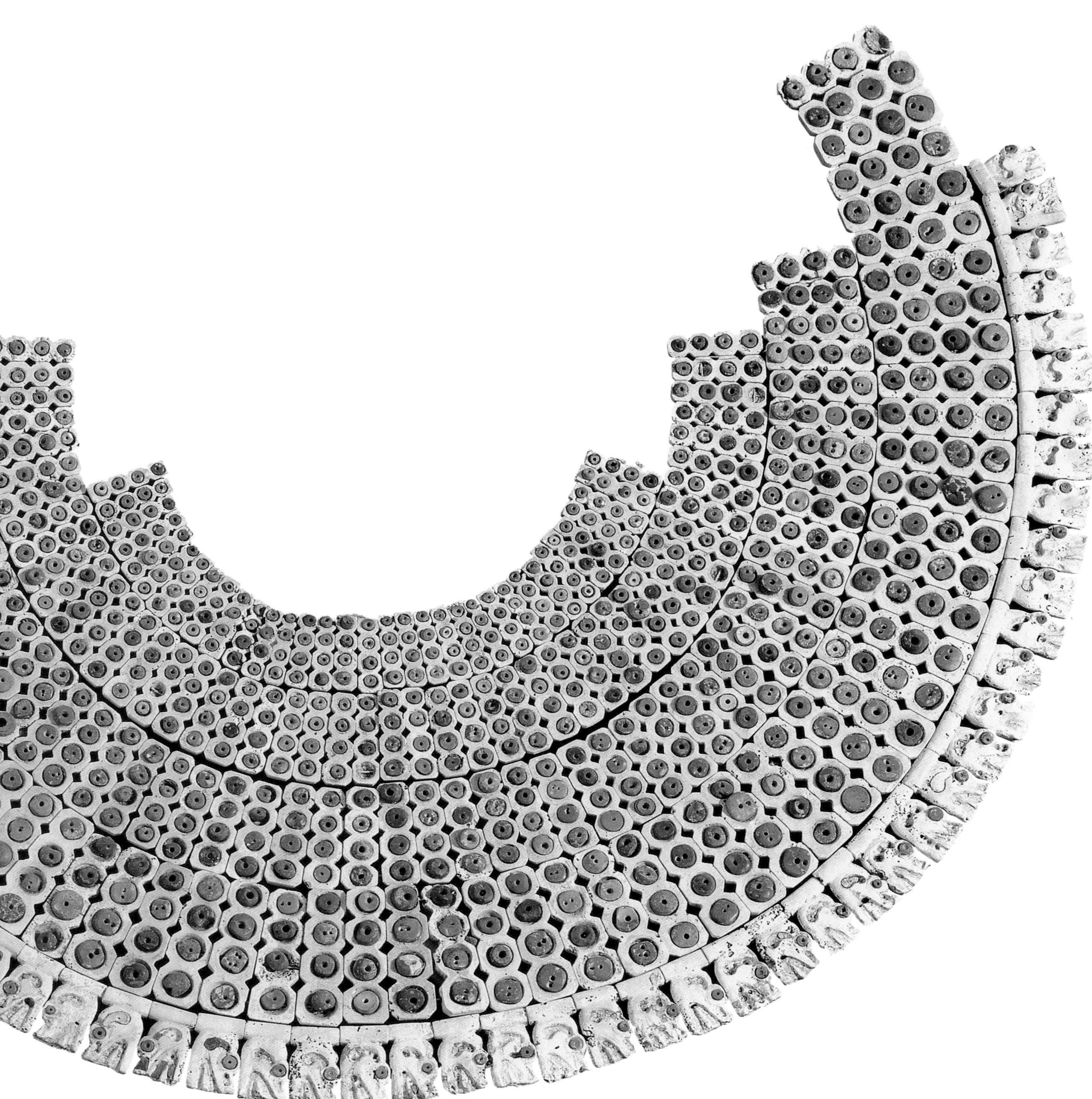

ABOVE
Paracas artists expressed Chavín symbolism in their own styles. On this Paracas pot an incised Chavín deity face is rendered in highly stylized geometric form. The post-fired, earth-toned paint is distinctive of early Paracas ceramics but the double spout-and-bridge form remained popular in the area for centuries.

build up the vessel. A wooden paddle was commonly used to pat the clay, with a smooth stone—the "anvil"—held in the other hand to keep the clay in place as it was patted. Although in many places the use of molds became common, especially among the Moche and others on the north coast (see illustration, page 19), on the south coast hand-building remained popular.

Paracas potters tended to treat their creations as canvases. They favored incision, as did Chavín potters, but the lines that they cut were filled in with deep, rich red, umber, and yellow paints with white, blue, or green generally used for highlights. Vessels were incised before firing and painted afterward, and the post-fired painting is a distinctive mark of Paracas pottery. Almost unique in the Andes is the Paracas use of paint mixed with a clotted resin, producing a thick appearance.

Paracas designs were highly abstract and geometrical; some are Chavín-like monster faces reduced to parallel lines, arcs, and circles. Modeling was used mostly for the depiction of the heads of birds or similar creatures adorning one of two spouts connected by a bridge of clay. This "double-spout-and-bridge" form was used elsewhere in the Andes but it was particularly popular on the south coast of Peru, and remained part of the stylistic repertoire for pottery of the highest status throughout most of Andean prehistory.

Late in the Paracas phase, a number of potters forsook the dense colors of post-fired painting for lighter effects. Some vessels, such as representations of squashes, were simply dipped before firing in a thin paint, or slip, that completely covered the surface. Other vessels were smoothed and their surfaces selectively decorated with wax or another substance before being slipped and fired. The slip would not adhere to the wax, and on the fired vessel the color of the original surface appears through the usually darker slip where the wax has melted, creating a "negative painting" effect.

CHAMBERS OF THE DEAD

In the gray and dun-colored landscape of the south coast more than polychrome ceramics brightened the lives of its ancient inhabitants. The Paracas peninsula today is a barren land with burning summers and fierce sandstorms. There are no rivers, no rain, and no plants. Starting in the Early Horizon, however, this inhospitable area became the site of a special mortuary center that has yielded some of the most beautiful creations of Andean artists. Beginning in 1925, Julio C. Tello excavated two cemeteries there, the Necrópolis de Wari Kayan, on Cerro Colorado, and Cabeza Larga (also known as Arena Blanca), less than a mile away. In both cemeteries two successive and related cultural groups buried their dead. The earlier group is known as

BELOW
The imposing, barren mass of the Paracas peninsula in southern Peru is a place for sealions, flamingos, and the dead. Swathed in fog and swept by winds, it still retains the aura of mystery and enchantment that drew peoples of the south coast there to inter their élite deceased in the cemeteries at Wari Kayan and Cabeza Larga.

LEFT

The figures on Paracas embroidered textiles have been interpreted as priests or shamans dressed to impersonate gods. This resin-painted Paracas mask may have been worn in such a ritual. Small holes around the mask's edge suggest that a cloth or cloak was sewn to it to hide the wearer.

RIGHT

Ceramic figurines are relatively rare in Paracas art. The closed eyes and mouth in this example may indicate that the person is dead and thus a revered ancestor. The large bib may represent cloth, or it is perhaps a stylized collar similar to the example illustrated on page 53.

Cavernas ("caverns") from its underground tomb chambers, which are accessible by a vertical shaft. Several individuals were buried in each tomb, accompanied by goods including the characteristic post-fired painted Paracas ceramics. Later burials, known as Necropolis burials, are distinctive for the sometimes huge "mummy bundles" of elaborately wrapped, flexed human corpses. These later shaft tombs are more sophisticated in design, often with a square or rectangular masonry chamber. The mummies were wrapped in a wealth of embroidered cloaks, mantles, tunics, and headdresses that has been described as possibly the richest find of ancient textiles in the world. Some of the ceramics that accompanied the Necropolis dead, in a style called Topará, prefigured the later Nasca style.

While the peninsula is arid, water is available beneath the desert surface, and there is evidence of human habitation near the cemetery sites. But whether the burials are of local people, or the peninsula was a special mortuary complex to which the dead were brought great distances, remains in dispute. What does seem certain is that the burials were wrapped in textiles and buried with goods that must have come from outside the peninsula itself. For example, some Paracas garments were woven with camelid wool (probably alpaca) from the highlands. So communication with other communities was taking place.

At present, however, little is known about the daily lives of these people, who were located primarily in the Chincha, Pisco, Ica, and Rio Grande de Nazca valleys. They do appear to have lived in a hierarchical society, perhaps with chiefs as leaders. The Paracas sites may have been special cemeteries for local lords, who were brought from their homes for burial. Their bodies were flexed in a sitting or squatting position, bound, and wrapped in several layers of cloth to create a

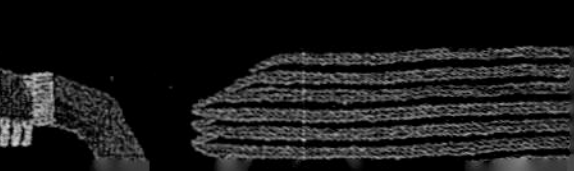

LEFT, ABOVE
Figures with mixed human and animal characteristics were popular in the Paracas "Block Color" style. This figure from a mantle is more human-like but has supernatural features in its face, snake belt, and long, serpent-like tongue. A staff is held in one hand and a fan or half-moon-shaped knife in the other (see also page 146).

LEFT, BELOW
These figures on a Paracas "Block Color" style mummy mantle seem to float past one another in a spiritual realm. While generally anthropomorphic, their twisted legs and protruding chests, as well as their bent-backward heads, are signs that identify them as supernaturals.

"mummy bundle." In the earlier Cavernas phase, tombs were often large, containing multiple burials surrounding a principal mummy bundle. These were probably family or clan groups of some kind. In the later cemetery large single bundles were entombed in specially constructed underground chambers.

PREPARING FOR THE AFTERLIFE

The Paracas mummies can be thought of as elaborate art constructions. The most elaborate, high-status, burials are close to 6ft (1.8m) high and more than 4ft (1.2m) in width and contain more than forty fancy cloths, dozens of plain cloths, other clothes, food offerings, and various items such as necklaces, pins, sewing baskets, and staffs. The flexed body was placed upright in a large shallow basket and wrapped in these many layers, and the entire construction was often further padded with cotton or leaves before being covered with a final, plain outer cover.

The mummy bundles contained some very fine textiles, the most remarkable being large mantles, some as big as 4ft by 9ft (1.2m by 2.75m), and occasionally twice this size or even larger. The mantles are extraordinary works of art, owing to the great amount of embroidery lavished upon them in two varieties, "Linear" style and the slightly later, though overlapping, "Block Color" style. The Linear style is characterized by parallel strips of embroidery against a dark background and within an elaborate border. Designs commonly feature large-eyed faces and felines in complex interlocking "S"-shaped patterns.

The Block Color style derives its name from the arrangement of distinct embroidered motifs in checkerboard and similarly spaced patterns against the background color. Unlike the Linear Style, the Block Color style employs quite clear images, at least in their general forms. They often portray a masked humanoid figure with an elaborate headdress and various appendages, including human heads. Much of the symbolism of these images appears to refer to fertility—especially the fertility

FOLLOWING PAGES
Double-headed, stylized birds and feline figures dominate the decorated border of this south coast Paracas mantle. It is made from camelid fibers, which absorb dye more readily than cotton.

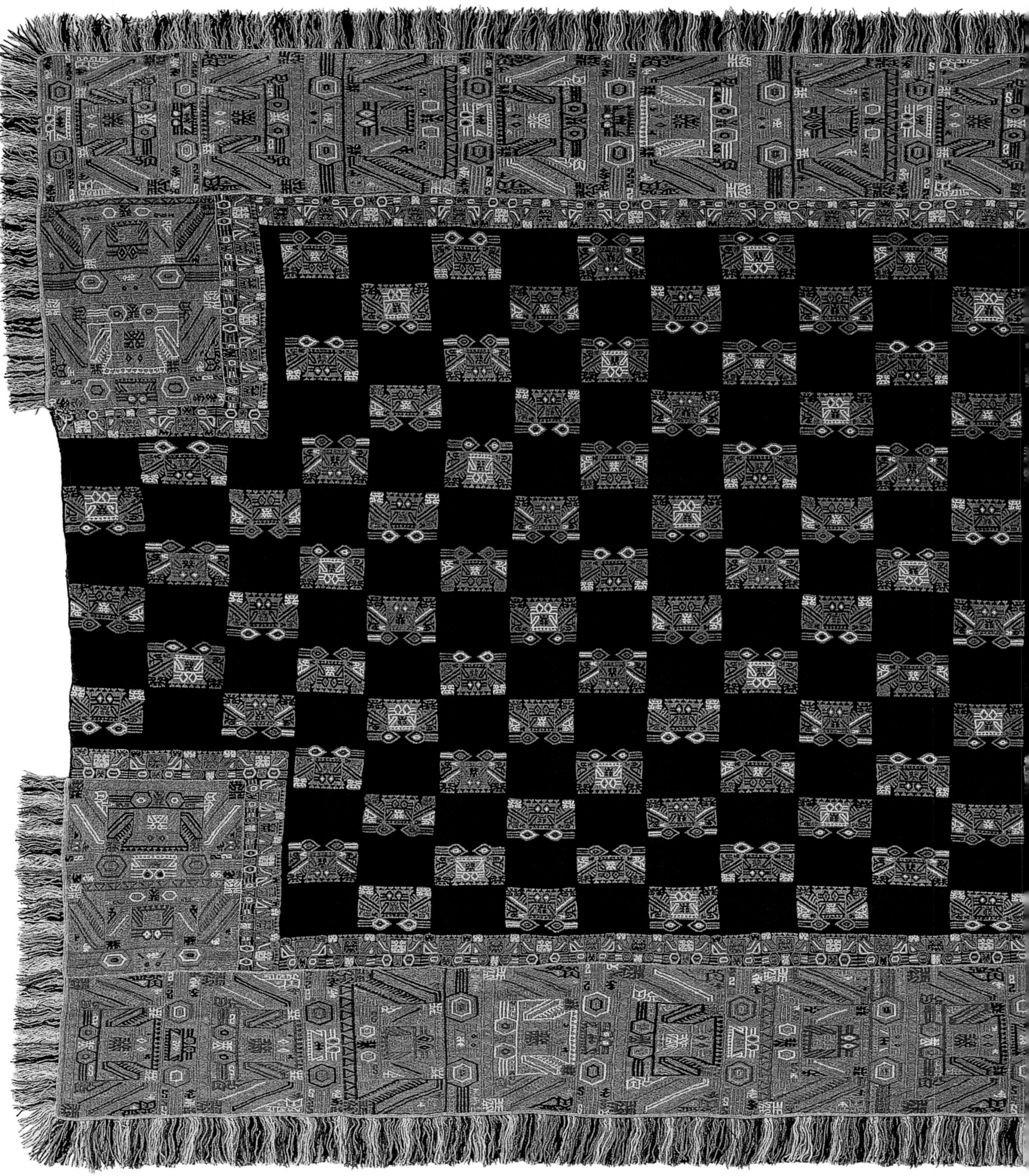

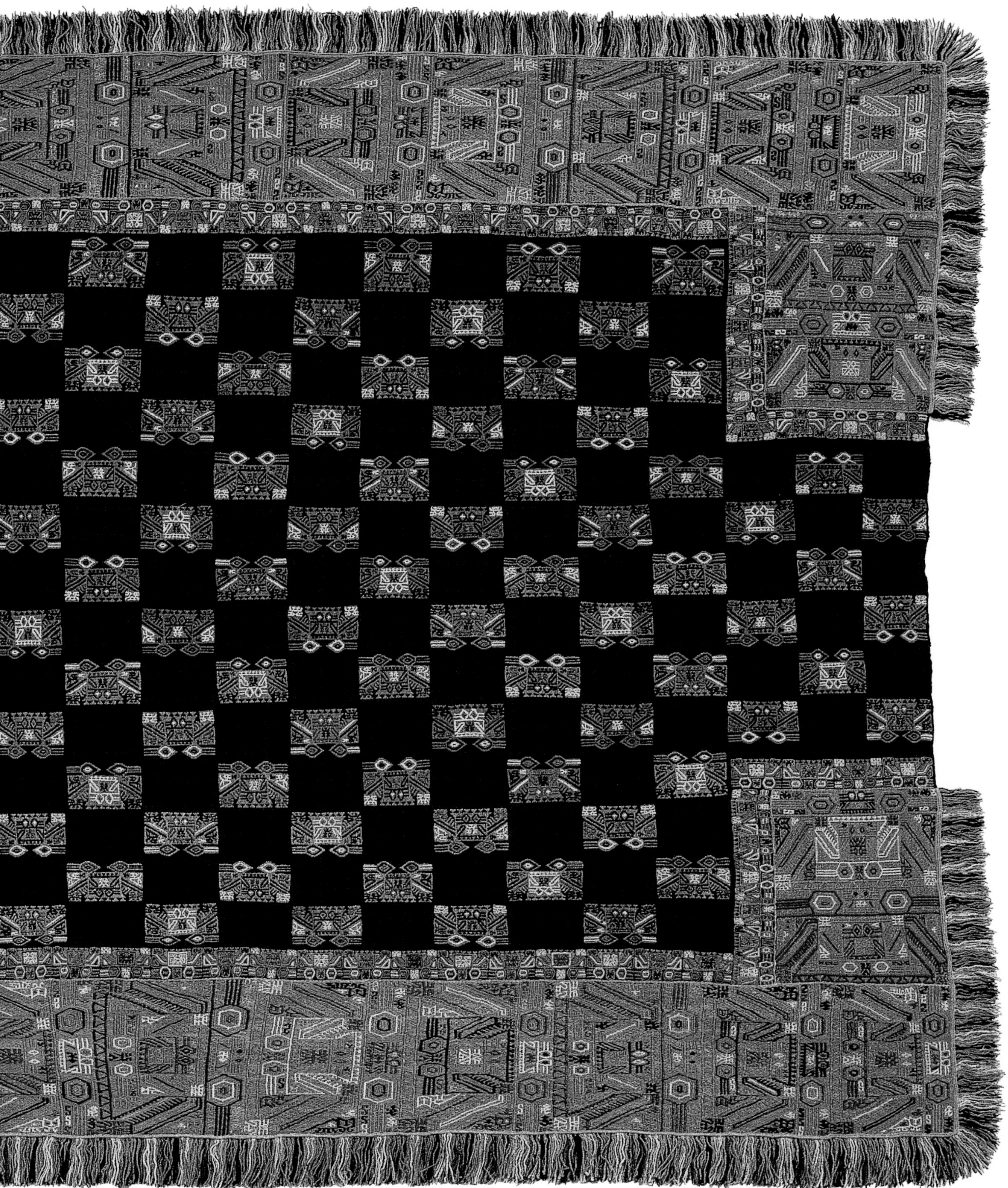

LEFT AND OPPOSITE
A strip of Paracas "Linear" style embroidery (detail opposite). Many such brilliantly colored bands would be set on a plain background with a matching elaborate border. The fabric shows a fantastic intermingling of images including supernatural beings, serpents, trophy heads and headdresses.

brought by life-giving water, a key concern in a dry region. Some figures sprout bean vines, while the motif of the severed head taken as a trophy in war—which was to prove particularly popular among the later Nasca people—was more a symbol of fertility and regeneration than of death. Indeed, the form of the whole mummy bundle itself appears to have represented a huge seed, with the kernel the flexed body of an ancestor, waiting to be born again—the food offerings and other personal items suggest that the Paracas people believed in an afterlife. Or, perhaps, the deceased was believed to emanate fertility to successive generations.

The stunning artistry of Paracas mantles is evident not only in the great amount of embroidery applied to each mantle but also in the complex way in which the overall design was planned and executed. The clothes and other regalia of the embroidered figures were systematically color-coordinated to produce patterns. Thus, for example, the color of one figure's tunic might be used in the headdress of the figure next to it, while the distinctive color combinations used in each figure might run diagonally across the entire textile.

Considering how many mantles were found in a single élite mummy bundle, a huge amount of labor went into the creation of a complete bundle. Unfinished textiles and "samplers"—practice pieces, probably the work of young women learning the techniques and images of their craft—have been found in some bundles, suggesting that the process of making funerary cloths was a long and involved one. One estimate puts the time required to create an elaborate mummy bundle at between 5,000 and 29,000 hours. Like Egyptian pharaohs, Paracas leaders may have had their households engaged in preparing the raiment for their afterlife long before their deaths.

The tradition of the Paracas mummy bundles spans the time between the late Early Horizon, toward the end of Chavín, and the first phases of the following era, the Early Intermediate Period. Soon a new style came to dominate the region, with its heartland in the Nazca River valley to the south of Paracas.

chapter 3

SACRED MOUNTAINS, SACRED PLAINS

THE EARLY INTERMEDIATE PERIOD

CA. 0CE–CA. 650CE

LEFT
Mists shroud the mountain peaks in the Andean foothills inland near the Nazca River valley, to the south of the Paracas peninsula where Nasca civilization had originated in the Paracas culture.

ART, WAR, AND SACRIFICE

THE RISE OF THE NASCA

Following the period of widespread artistic and cultural unity of the Early Horizon, the Paracas peoples steered a course that led their art away from the Chavín styles that had originally inspired it. The Paracas style persisted into the following era of Andean cultural history, the Early Intermediate Period, and then declined. At this time, more than a hundred miles (160km) farther south, a new cultural style emerged in the Nazca River valley. The art of the Nasca people was among the most dynamic and beautiful ever produced in the Andes.

We know little about the lives of Nasca common folk but it appears that many of their elaborate ceramics and textiles were created by local craftspeople in small villages and hamlets. The huge architectural complex of Cahuachi, covering 0.6 sq miles (1.5sq km), was once thought to be the mighty capital of a Nasca state. However, research has suggested that many of the forty mounds from the heyday of its occupation were natural hills that were modified to appear to be artificial constructions. Helaine Silverman suggests that Cahuachi was mostly an empty ceremonial center, with only a small resident population. Most people would have lived in the countryside, from where they visited Cahuachi in community groups to celebrate rituals. The Nasca probably put as much, or more, effort into building long subterranean conduits in order to bring water to normally dry areas lower in the valley. Areas serviced by such tunnels, which were dug into aquifers (natural underground water channels) to catch surface water run-off, were densely populated and farmed. Water was a central concern of peoples in the arid coastal regions, and one theory has linked the famous "Nasca Lines" of this area with a cult aimed at bringing water to the dry parts of the valley (see pages 74–77).

LEFT
Nasca ceramic pan pipes, with their binding and decorative cloth straps preserved by the desert sands. Especially popular among the Nasca and Moche, pan pipes were made in a variety of sizes.

RIGHT
The Nasca interest in heads, which led them to take trophy heads in war, also manifested in special treatment for their own dead, hence this elaborately crowned mortuary remain.

LEFT
Part of the success of the Nasca was owing to their skillful manipulation of water resources such as these cisterns, which tapped underground water channels at Cahuachi, the Nasca ritual center. The stone-lined spiral ramp may have had religious significance but was also an efficient way to reach great depths and enable heavy jars of water to be carried out.

LEFT
Garments of colorful tropical bird feathers attached to cloth were among the most valued possessions of peoples in ancient Peru. The stylized monkey or human on this brilliant Nasca garment is an unusual figure, but it is one with vibrant impact.

BELOW
This Nasca effigy jar in the "Proliferous" style depicts a man with a stylized cat-whisker mask and a headdress. The trophy heads across his shoulders and dangling from his neck indicate his status as a high-ranking warrior.

A WEALTH OF COLOR

Nasca artists reveled in the exuberant use of a rich and varied color palette. For approximately seven centuries—through to about 600CE—Nasca potters mastered painting thin slip on unfired vessels through eight distinct stylistic phases. When they attained the zenith of their craft, somewhere around the middle of these phases, they used as many as thirteen colors to decorate a single pot.

All images were outlined in black, perhaps echoing the Paracas penchant for incision, but there is a distinct pattern of change in Nasca ceramics through time. Early "Proto-Nasca" (or Nasca phase 1) ceramics retain the thick paints of the earlier style as well as incising. In "Monumental" Nasca works (phases 2–4), a single animal or mythical being might decorate the bottom of a plate or shallow bowl, or there might be a procession of a few animals around the outer surface of a deeper vessel. The succeeding "Proliferous" sub-styles bore increasingly crowded imagery on pottery surfaces. Motifs, which also changed through time, included increasingly militaristic themes such as warriors, trophy heads (human heads taken in warfare as trophies), and gods or god impersonators (priests or shamans dressed as deities and performing rituals). These latter two sometimes consist of multiple faces or masks linked together by long, sinuous tongues or, perhaps reflecting trophy heads, long lines and bands of rope.

The Nasca were noted for their textiles and goldwork and gold ritual implements have been found that are also depicted in art. Also, pan pipes, which were widely in use by the middle Early Horizon era, became highly popular among the Nasca (see page 66) and today are emblematic of Andean music.

BELOW
A roll-out image of the decorated side of a bowl in the "Proliferous" style emphasizes the Nasca obsession with trophy heads. The varied skin colors depicted may not simply be decoration but attest to the wide range of enemies defeated in battle.

THE POWER OF THE HEAD

Trophy heads were prized among the Nasca (see illustrations below and on pages 67 and 71) and seem to have been symbolically tied to the idea of sources of fertility, like seeds. The head received other attentions as well. The Nasca and other people of the south coast were particularly fond of altering the shape of a child's head by binding it on a cradleboard in infancy. As the child grew, its head would acquire a distinctive shape, apparently with no effect to the functioning of the brain. The evidence from graves has revealed many styles of deliberate head deformation in ancient Peru; slanted foreheads and conical shapes appear to have been especially popular. Other evidence of a concern with heads was the practice of trephination, or trepanning,

RIGHT
A pair of naked figurines carved from whalebone with headdresses of colored shell. They may once have sported elaborate costumes. The slanted forehead shape favored by the Nasca was created by binding the head in infancy.

again particularly popular on the south coast. This practice involved deliberately making holes in the skull and exposing the brain. The discovery of skulls with healed wounds show that the patient commonly survived this procedure—often to have it repeated several more times.

Some of these operations were performed to cure head wounds probably inflicted in warfare while others may have been attempts to remedy diseases believed to originate in the brain. But often there is no clear reason at all; one theory has suggested that trepanning may have been performed in order to induce visions.

LINES IN THE DESERT

Among the most remarkable examples of ancient landscape architecture in the New World are the desert markings of the south coast of Peru. They are found in many places but are concentrated on the Pampa de Nazca. The "Nasca Lines," as they are known (after the culture), have attracted much speculation, some of it sensationalist, as to their origins and purposes. However, Nasca-style shards of pottery have been found next to the lines, and wooden stakes that were used to lay out the designs have been radiocarbon-dated to Nasca times. All the evidence supports the logical theory—that the lines were made by local inhabitants. Two people, with sticks, string, simple sighting devices, and brooms could have produced many of the lines by simply moving cobbles and brushing away the dark surface soil to reveal the lighter-colored soil below.

RIGHT AND BELOW
There are hundreds of lines in the Pampa de Nazca but only about 30 figures, such as the hummingbird shown here (right). The hummingbird, also depicted on the Nasca vessel below, was appreciated for its aggressiveness and swiftness. These are ideal characteristics of warriors, thus apparently benign scenes such as these may have carried a deeper and more militant symbolic meaning.

The lines are concentrated along a 6-mile (10-km) area overlooking a nearby river. They were made over a two thousand-year period and this, coupled with the fact that there are many different kinds of lines and that they often overlap, has made their investigation difficult. The images include figural renderings of animals and plants (monkey, spider, killer whale, hummingbird, flower). There are also geometric and abstract forms and simple straight lines, sometimes emanating from "ray centers" and stretching for several miles. Some of the lines are too large to be viewed in their entirety from the ground or even nearby hills, but many others can easily be seen from local uplands.

RITUAL PATHWAYS AND WATER CULTS

It is highly likely that different styles of line were made for different purposes over the many centuries of their creation on the Pampa de Nazca. It has been proposed that the figural depictions represent an astronomical calendar, but there is no firm evidence to support this theory. The fact that the images were made with continuous lines that never cross one another has suggested to some scholars that

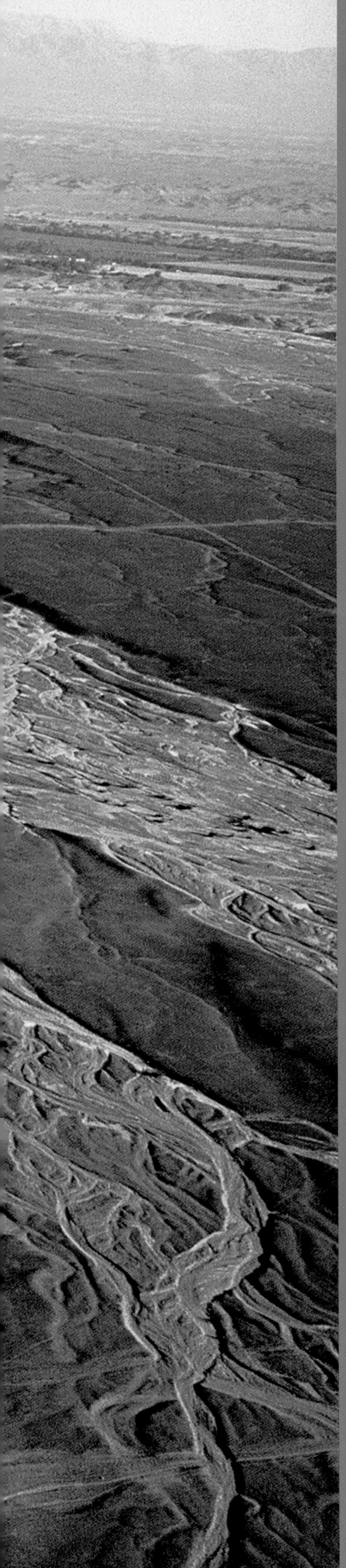

they, as well as some of the straight lines, may have been used as ritual pathways, similar to the labyrinths used for meditation in medieval churches, which were representations of the road to Jerusalem. Indeed, one of the Nasca markings is labyrinthine, consisting of a spiral which, if walked, leads one from the outside into the heart of the design and back out again, all on the same line.

Anthony F. Aveni and his colleagues have proposed that the lines and geometrical designs were used for rituals to bring water from the mountains to the valley. They were able to document 62 ray centers and 750 associated lines that extend for over 77 sq miles (200sq km). Many of these were located on natural rises, at the bottom of mountains and above stream beds, leading Aveni and his colleagues to conclude that the lines and ray centers were connected with a water cult. Such cults were naturally popular in the desert, and droughts and floods brought by El Niño played a crucial role not only in Andean religion but also in the rise and fall of entire cultures.

LEFT
The most common form of Pampa de Nazca markings are straight lines and geometric designs such as this spectacular expanding trapezoid. Made over centuries, they likely have various meanings and purposes, depending on when they were made.

ABOVE
The giant image of a monkey is one of the most well known of the desert markings. It is of particular interest because it depicts a tropical forest animal in the barren desert. Perhaps south coast peoples kept such exotic creatures in captivity.

LORDS OF THE NORTH

THE MOCHE AND THEIR WORLD

OPPOSITE
The principal deity of the Moche is represented by this double-fanged polychrome frieze at the Huaca de La Luna at Cerro Blanco, the Moche capital. It is only recently that brightly colored Moche friezes and murals have been uncovered in quantity.

The trajectory taken by the peoples of the north coast of Peru following the disintegration of Chavín was in a completely different direction from that of their contemporaries in the south. Whereas Paracas and Nasca artists reveled in rich colors in their ceramics and textiles, those of the Salinar and Gallinazo cultures of the north coast continued the Chavín tradition (also practiced by the culture known as Cupisnique) of highly polished pottery in a single, usually light, color.

However, little is known about the Salinar and Gallinazo cultures other than their surviving ceramics. The troubled times that followed the Chavín are signaled, perhaps, by exquisitely made Salinar maceheads carved out of a single block of stone. Blades and spikes were creatively combined on these maceheads to produce

RIGHT
The huge platform mound at Cerro Blanco now known as the Huaca del Sol. At one time smooth and brightly painted, it has been eroded by centuries of El Niño rains and looters. More than 100 million adobe bricks were used in what was one of the largest mounds ever built in the New World.

OPPOSITE
A Moche metalwork figure of an owl. The Moche associated coastal owls with the dead and the underworld, possibly due to their habit of burrowing in the soft earth of ancient mounds. As predators, owls were also respected as exemplary warriors.

monumental objects, despite their small size. Nicks on some of the mace-heads suggest that they may actually have been used in armed combat.

Centered in the Viru River valley, Gallinazo was the first culture to build huge complexes of raised adobe platforms. Earlier ceremonial centers had been variations on the U-plan architecture of the later Preceramic Period and early Initial Period (see Chapter 1), with occasional raised platforms. In the Early Intermediate Period, however, ceremonial centers on the north coast began to take the basic form of a single temple with a large plaza fronting it. Interestingly, many sites had two such temples, perhaps continuing the idea of dualism. Many of the temples were huge, consisting of stacked platforms resembling the ziggurats of the ancient Near East.

THE RISE OF THE MOCHE

Gallinazo appears to have been earlier than the famous Moche culture and to have originated many practices continued by it. However, recent research suggests that Gallinazo populations and practices may have continued for a considerable time alongside the new cults and culture of the Moche, eventually being absorbed into them.

The Moche arose in the Moche and Chicama river valleys around the beginning of the Common Era, and came to dominate the whole of the north coast. Like the Chavín they took old ideas and reworked them and added something new. However, if the Chavín cult was based on mystery, on meeting the gods deep in the heart of the temple, the Moche

ABOVE
The attachment holes at the top of this feline mask, with its dramatic fangs of bone which suggest that it is an image of the Moche principal deity, indicate it may once have been part of a larger object. The green oxidation indicates that the object, which may have had a ritual purpose, possesses a high copper content. Copper-gold alloy was common, with higher gold content usually reserved for more precious items.

brought their gods out into the open, performing grisly sacrificial rites in plain view on the summits of their temples, but at a distance from the crowds below.

BLOOD ON THE TEMPLE TOP

The crowd had gathered in the plaza in front of the great terraced Moche temple. It was the hottest time of day when they at last saw the puffs of dust in the distance that signaled the arrival of the warriors and their prisoners. The plaza walls prevented a good view, but finally they entered the plaza at a brisk pace. The first warriors, except for the standard-bearer, carried long wooden clubs onto which were tied the clothing, helmets, shields, and other regalia of their prisoners. One warrior held the end of a long rope that stretched backwards and around the necks of ten prisoners, all running to prevent strangling one another. There were thirty prisoners in all, bound together

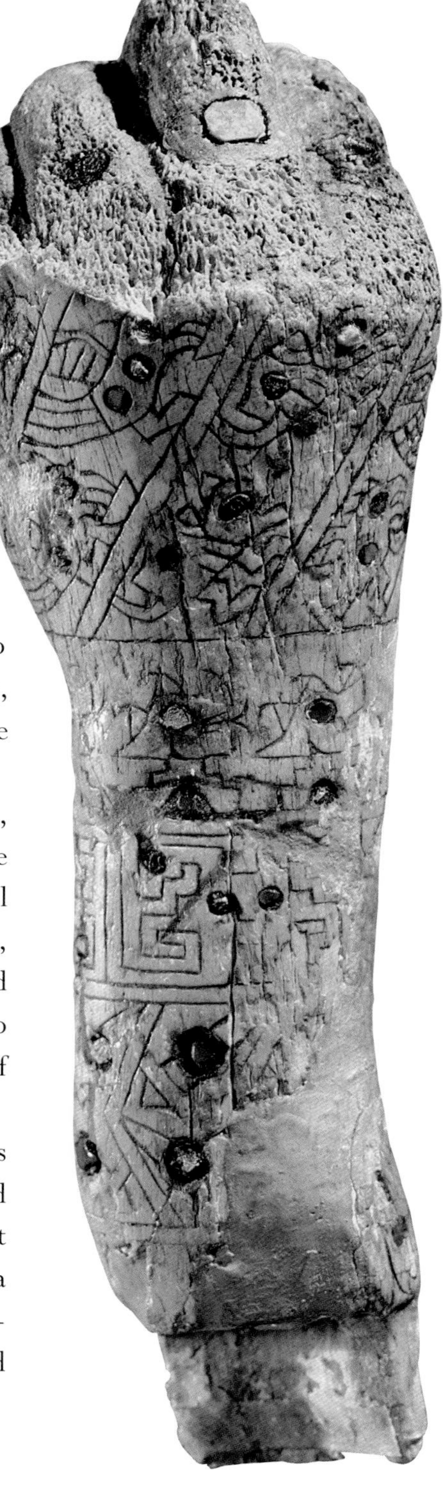

BELOW
A Moche bone spatula handle carved in the shape of a closed fist imitating mountain peaks associated with ritual sacrifices. The incisions depict war clubs, stressing the martial theme.

in groups of ten. The captives were all men, aged between about eighteen and thirty-five and naked except for the tattoos on their upper bodies and smudged war paint on their lower legs. Their hair was tousled and the onlookers could see that many had broken noses. They were bleeding at their fingertips where the nails had been torn out, and some had bloody genitals.

After circling the plaza to the cheers of the crowd, warriors and prisoners ran by the wall of the lowest terrace of the temple. For a moment, the living blur of men matched perfectly the frieze on the wall behind them which portrayed, life-size, a similar grisly parade. On the terrace above them, a line of temple priests, dressed all in orange, held hands and bellowed out a sacred chant and they too matched the scene depicted on the wall of the next terrace above them. Higher up, successive terraces portrayed the Spider God and other fearsome members of the Moche pantheon.

Within minutes the warriors had led the prisoners into the temple complex, and as the orange-clad priests filed in too, the crowd below waited for the next scene to unfold. The top of the Huaca had no wall but at its far left end there was a small stepped platform. As if from nowhere, a warrior-priest appeared on the platform, dressed in gold—a shirt of solid gold plates, a huge gold back-flap, and a large gold crown. To the people in the plaza the sunlight reflected off his dress seemed to emanate from his very being as he stood, tall and in profile, looking along the top of the temple toward the scene before him.

Three of the prisoners were then brought out onto the temple top, their hands bound behind their backs. Quickly, another priest stepped forward, raised a curved knife, and slashed deep into the jugular vein of one of the prisoners. A priestess bent to catch the gushing blood in a chalice. Once filled, the chalice was covered with a plate and the priestess and other priests processed to the raised platform. They presented the cup to the warrior-priest, who raised it high, then brought it to his lips and

RIGHT

This spectacular metal figure, more than 2ft (60cm) long, was found with the Old Lord of Sipán, a high-ranking Moche noble. The feline-faced deity either did not continue in later times or was transformed in its representation. The double-snake head emblem did continue, and may represent the surface of the heavenly plane.

BELOW

Moche ceramics commonly show deer as war captives, a status indicated on this jar by the seated position and the rope. Deer hunting and human warfare are often closely associated in many Pre-Columbian cultures.

drained it. The crowds below uttered cries of praise at this act, which told them that the sun had been nourished and the continuous cycle of the cosmos maintained.

RITES OF SACRIFICE

As in the story of the pilgrim at Chavín de Huantar (see pages 36–39), this imagined account of a Moche sacrificial ritual is based upon detailed evidence, such as the paintings on the walls of temples and scenes depicted on ceramics. The Old Lord of Sipán, whose rich burial was one of the most spectacular archaeological discoveries in the Andes, was a high-ranking Moche who had played the role of the warrior-priest who received the cup of blood. Numerous art works portray a priestess in the act of presenting the cup, and burials of women arrayed in the same costume as such a priestess have been discovered at the site of San José de Moro.

The identity of the prisoners depicted in temple murals and the circumstances of their capture remain a matter of debate. Some scholars believe that the captives were taken in real warfare, while others believe that the ritual was staged more as ceremony, with the sacrificial victims drawn from the same population as those who performed the sacrifice. The ritual itself was probably carried out in order to guarantee fertility for crops, animals, and people. The Moche performed other sacrifices too, for example when the El Niño rains brought devastation to coastal dwellers. Who were the rulers and priests who erected these great temples and demanded such bloody ceremonies? Again, views are divided. Some scholars believe that Moche was a single, expansive imperialist state, based on the capital of

LEFT
The distinctive facial features on this Moche stirrup spout vessel, with its accompanying pair of raptor birds, suggest that it may be a true portrait. But it is not known whether the figure represents a historic or mythical individual or if a god is depicted.

Cerro Blanco in the Moche River valley, with its great temples, the Huaca del Sol and Huaca de la Luna. Others hold that the northern Moche were a separate region of Moche culture. Still others believe that there were several distinct political units, like city-states, in each valley of the 500-mile (800km) stretch of Peru's north coast where Moche cultural styles prevailed.

MYTH, SEX, AND RITUAL: MOCHE ART

Whatever their political systems may have been, the Moche, or Mochica, are one of the most artistically renowned cultures of the ancient Andes. In contrast to the Nasca, their pottery was usually decorated with only two colors, white-cream and buff-brown, but they employed these to great effect, using molds (see illustration, page 19) to create three-dimensional pieces and, later, employing fine line painting on vessel surfaces. Using these techniques, Moche artists depicted warriors, deities, plants, and animals. They showed houses and temples, battles and rituals, mythological scenes, and craftspeople at their trades. Sacrificial victims about to meet their death were also represented, as was sex, not only between humans but also between a host of different animals.

For more than a century, this marvelous art has delighted museum visitors, archaeologists, and collectors. It was only in the 1970s, however, that scholars began to observe that what appeared to be scenes of everyday life were actually infused with symbolic meaning. The portrayal of a deer or sealion hunt was not simply a depiction of a quest for food but was linked to notions of sacrifice and ritual. Deer seem to be analogues for humans, as they also were among the Maya in Mesoamerica, perhaps because they competed for food, browsing in maize fields (see illustration, page 84).

ABOVE
A running warrior depicted in an inlaid mosaic of lapis lazuli and shell adorns a large Moche ear spool made out of gold. Military themes vary through Andean prehistory but ear spools remain constant as emblems of high-ranking males: the larger the spool, the higher the rank. This view is of the large front of the spool; the shaft, which passed through the ear of the wearer, was smaller than this roundel and is located behind it.

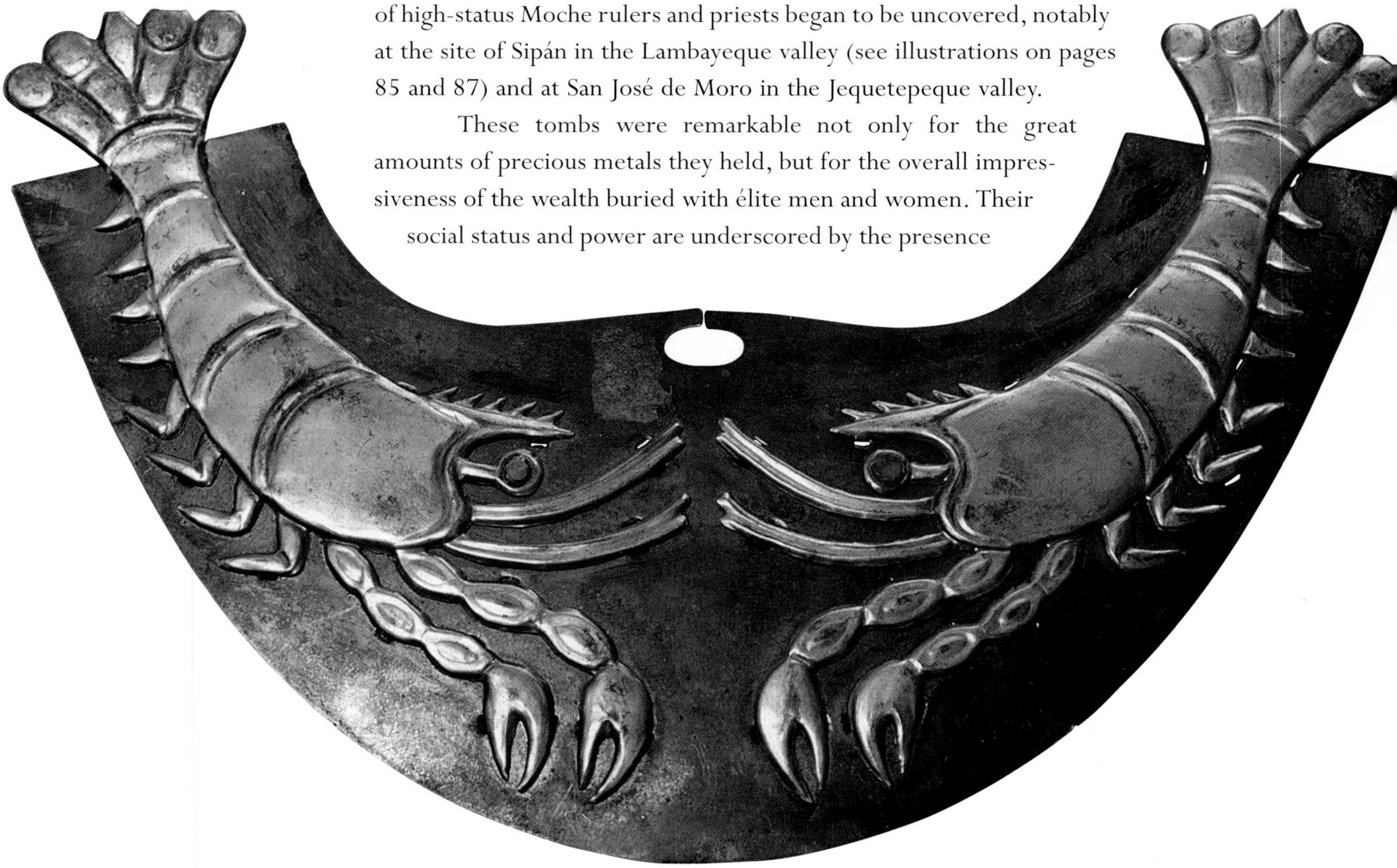

BELOW
Nose ornaments were popular among the Moche and their Ecuadorian neighbors. One as large as this would have covered the mouth and moved as the wearer spoke, probably adding to his aura of authority. It is unclear what the shellfish symbolized.

Sealions seem to have been ritually hunted to obtain the smooth stones that they ingest to aid digestion. The Moche apparently saw these as having magical properties.

ART FOR THE ÉLITE

Just as the Greek gods acted like humans and were portrayed in human form, the Moche conceived of their deities as very much like themselves in their clothing and activities. The links between the mythological world of the Moche gods and that of humans were confirmed from the mid-1980s, when the spectacular tombs of high-status Moche rulers and priests began to be uncovered, notably at the site of Sipán in the Lambayeque valley (see illustrations on pages 85 and 87) and at San José de Moro in the Jequetepeque valley.

These tombs were remarkable not only for the great amounts of precious metals they held, but for the overall impressiveness of the wealth buried with élite men and women. Their social status and power are underscored by the presence

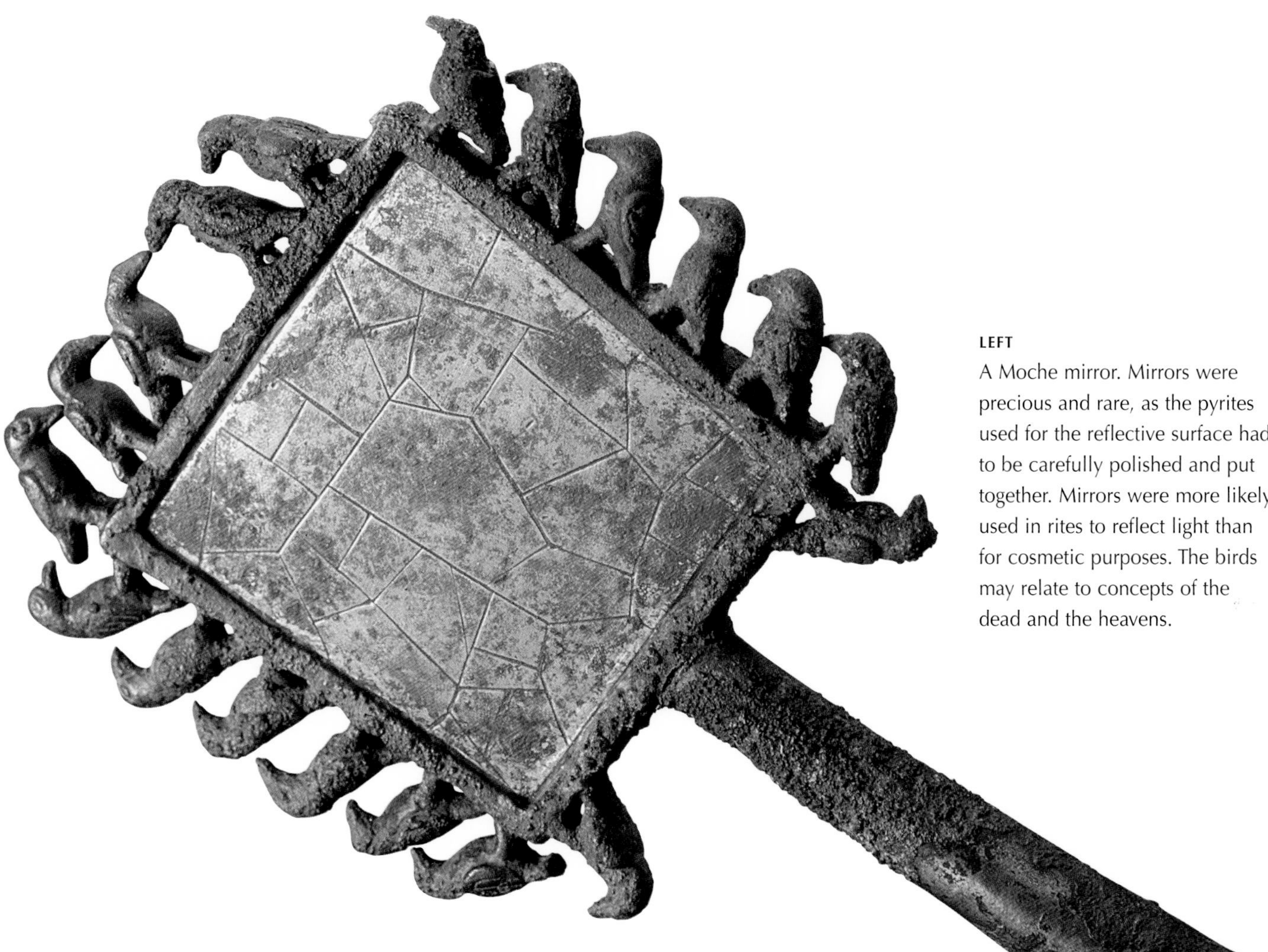

LEFT
A Moche mirror. Mirrors were precious and rare, as the pyrites used for the reflective surface had to be carefully polished and put together. Mirrors were more likely used in rites to reflect light than for cosmetic purposes. The birds may relate to concepts of the dead and the heavens.

in the tombs of sacrificed retainers. Even more important, perhaps, is that the remains discovered in these tombs made it clear that scenes portrayed in art were not only mythological events but were enacted by living people, costumed as gods, in Moche rituals and festivals. The tombs of priestesses suggests that at least some women were able to attain high status in Moche society. Whether they participated in broader political activities or were confined to religious roles is hard to determine, but evidence of high-status women is also found in figurines, and there are other subtle indicators that they had important roles to play outside of strictly religious roles.

Curiously, the Moche were the only people in prehistoric South America to render the faces of living people in art, in their famous "portrait vases" (see illustration, page 86). There is little doubt that these masterpieces were modeled on real people, but it is hard to ascertain if they were intended as portraits of the living individuals or as representations of mythological heroes or minor deities.

Although Andean artisans are now known to have produced metal objects as early as the Initial Period, the Moche took metalworking technology to new heights. They made elaborate jewelry and costume elements from hammered sheet metal and

practiced complex lost-wax casting. Moche craftspeople made sophisticated alloys of gold, silver, and copper in different combinations. Sometimes, they inlaid precious metal with spondylus shells and with semiprecious stones, such as lapis lazuli, that may have come from as far away as Chile.

OPPOSITE
The Moche particularly favored the use of alternating patterns and colors, as in these elaborate ear spools combining snail shell, turquoise, and gold. Lizards were probably admired for their swiftness.

THE END OF THE MOCHE

After five or more centuries of cultural developments on the north coast of Peru, the gods of the Moche had become fierce and much of their art portrayed violence. Sacrifice is a common theme throughout Moche art but it took on a particularly vicious and more realistic character near the end of the style. The depiction of the march of naked prisoners on ceramic vessels and in wall friezes at temples suggests that abstract concepts of the symbiotic relationship of life and death had been replaced by darker themes of the sacrifice of prisoners from real conflicts. Such warfare was probably the result of demographic pressures brought on by growing populations, limited land and water for agriculture—and the upsetting of a delicate balance between these factors by devastating El Niño rains that appear to have occurred in late Moche times.

A MULTICULTURAL WORLD

The Nasca and the Moche are perhaps the best known of many regional cultures that emerged in the Andes in the Early Intermediate Period (ca.0CE–650CE). In many other regions different art styles and cultural practices grew to dominate local practices. Even in the Moche realm, two art styles or cultures appear to have existed alongside the better known Moche style. One is Gallinazo (see pages 78–79) and the other is Vicús, concentrated only in the upper Piura River valley, isolated from the Moche, farther south, by the Sechura Desert. The ransacking of numerous Vicús sites for gold work has made it difficult to study this culture except through museum collections. Vicús ceramics demonstrate a playfulness in depicting human forms in a

ABOVE
This double-chambered vessel and its negative-painted decoration are typically Vicús in style. The man peering out of his house may have deep symbolism, but Vicús pottery tends to appear more playful and commonplace than Moche art, with its serious and often macabre themes of war and fierce gods.

manner similar to Ecuadorian styles, farther north. As with the craft techniques later favored by the peoples or culture known to us as Paracas, when decorating vessels the Vicús appear to have been fond of "negative painting" techniques (see page 54), which allowed the color of the base clay to play an important part in the final appearance of the ceramic piece.

DEPICTING EVERYDAY LIFE: RECUAY

In the highlands, close to the area where Chavín once held sway, the Recuay style also emerged. Recuay artists appear to have been the first to fully embrace and celebrate the depiction of ordinary human beings carrying out ordinary daily activities. There is no pretense in figures portrayed in a limited color palette of black, white, and red-brown paint, which was applied to distinctive white kaolin (china clay) vessels. The Recuay, so called from a town of that name in the upper Santa River valley, shared with the Moche a preference for three-dimensional modeling. Depictions include gatherings of men and women in houses and ceremonial structures, high-ranking personages taking drinks, and other individuals shown standing alongside llamas.

RIGHT
The Recuay arose close to the old Chavín heartlands but seemed deliberately to reject the baroque earlier style in favor of simplicity. This figure may be an ancestor; many other figures depict warriors, which suggests unstable times.

It is perhaps the absence of fierce gods and angry deities that most characterizes Recuay ceramics rather than their emphasis on human affairs. The Recuay shared much with their coastal neighbors, the Moche, and likely were friends at some times and enemies at others during the centuries of their coexistence. The "Moon Animal" is one apparently minor deity that both cultures had in common. Otherwise, however, the finest Recuay ceramic art seems to represent high-ranking men and, notably, women—as among the Moche, Recuay women seem to have played an important role in Recuay culture as priestesses and shamans—engaged in ritual and everyday activities.

THE BREADBASKET OF THE ANDES

Another art style and culture, Lima, also arose in the Early Intermediate Period in one of the richest valley systems on the central coast of Peru. Here, the broad irrigated plains of the Chillón, Rimac, and Lurín rivers provided the population with a wealth of food. The Lima culture takes its name from the Peruvian capital, the name of which is itself a corruption of the Rimac, the river near which the city stands. Lima art generally does not garner much attention, and the sprawling metropolis has destroyed and overrun many of the culture's sites. However, very large and impressive temple mounds may still be seen in the parks of the modern city. The Lima left another great monument to posterity in the southernmost of the three valleys, the Lurín. Here, they elaborated an ancient temple complex that was known at the time of the Spanish conquest as Pachacamac. Its oracle and cult came to play an increasingly important role in the turbulent times that lay ahead (see pages 128–131).

RIGHT
This masterwork of gold inlaid with shell depicts the principal deity of the Moche. In addition to the fanged mouth, the double ear spools are a distinctive characteristic of the god.

ABOVE
This unusual Lima-style vessel shows influences from the south, in its double-spout and bridge form, and the highlands, in its snarling feline imagery. Elaborate spouts that were difficult to fill or pour from suggest that such vessels were made for purposes other than utilitarian ones.

ZENITH AND DECLINE

The Early Intermediate Period appears to have had three distinct phases. At the beginning there was a time of instability in the wake of the fall of Chavín. The second phase began around the fourth century CE, when the Nasca, Moche, and the other distinctive regional cultures discussed above reached their height, where they remained for at least two centuries.

During this period of maximum stability, these different cultures appear to have coexisted in relative peace. The people of the south coast were able to utilize the wool of camelids (llama, alpaca, and related species), possibly imported from the highlands, to weave their rich fabrics. Moche artisans used semiprecious stones that may have come from as far away as Chile. This and other evidence suggests that there were increasing connections between one region and another and beyond.

But this world stumbled, faltered, and then fell. It appears that environmental disasters combined with other factors began to destabilize these cultures from the sixth century CE. The cultures may have been victims of their own success, stretching to their limits the capacities of the coastal river valleys and highland agricultural terraces to support them. Severe El Niño events can produce massive deluges on the coast and prolonged droughts in the highlands. Such environmental shifts over lengthy periods could have severely crippled societies living at the edges of the sustainable limits of their ecological systems and technological capabilities.

At different rates and in slightly different ways, the Early Intermediate Period cultures gradually began to disintegrate or to be radically transformed by the forces of new ideas and peoples from the southern highlands of Peru and the high *altiplano* of Bolivia. This set the stage for the Middle Horizon of Andean prehistory.

chapter 4

LORDS OF HIGH PLACES

THE MIDDLE HORIZON

CA. 650–1000CE

LEFT

Detail of the "Gateway God" in the center of the carving on the Sun Gate, Tiwanaku. Many characteristics of the figure resemble the Chavín Staff God but it may be a different deity, perhaps a sun god. (See also pages 106–107.)

TIWANAKU AND WARI

MIGHTY POWERS OF THE HIGHLANDS

BELOW
A Pukará pot with engraved and painted decor plus a feline head. Pukará pottery was similar to Paracas ceramics in its use of different colors outlined by incision. The feline motif may be Chavín-related or part of a shared tradition, because Pukará was outside of Chavín's direct sphere of influence.

In the era known as the Middle Horizon, a vast area of the Andean landscape came under the influence of highland powers for the second time in prehistory. The Middle Horizon dates to between approximately 650CE and 1000CE, the period of greatest unity, when the cities of Tiwanaku and Huari were at their most powerful and influential. However, the social and cultural changes that led to this dominance were well underway in the south highlands long before this time.

If Chavín missionaries had ever traveled to the southern highlands and the high plains, the *altiplano*, they were not well received, for the locals maintained their own ancient traditions. On the southern shore of Lake Titicaca, in present-day Bolivia, a platform mound faced with stone was constructed in about 1000BCE at the site of Chiripa, which dates to the Initial Period. Sometime between around 600BCE and 100BCE this monument boasted a sunken court, also stone-faced and surrounded by sixteen small rectangular buildings. The arrangement suggests a system not unlike that of the Kotosh religious tradition, in which extended families each had their own representative shrine at a central place (see Chapter 1).

Elsewhere around the Titicaca Basin there were early ceramic traditions that differed from Chiripa, but the peoples of the basin shared similar conventions of stone carving and ceremonial structures. These shared cultural practices, and the religious beliefs that have been inferred from them, have been called the Yaya-Mama religious tradition. Some of the general features of the architecture appear to have been the foundations for later Tiwanaku practices. Tiwanaku people apparently revered the ancestral Yaya-Mama tradition since they included some of the older culture's sculpture in their ceremonial complexes.

Around 400BCE, during the Early Horizon period, on the Peruvian side of Lake Titicaca, the Yaya-Mama tradition appears to have

RIGHT
A Pukará stele, possibly a depiction of a skeletonized *suche*, a freshwater fish of the *altiplano*.This low relief is typical of Yaya-Mama style in its loose, flowing treatment of the image.

been elaborated by south coast design influences. The site of Pukará spreads over several miles and on the summit of a hill there is a ceremonial precinct with a sunken court surrounded by small structures that is reminiscent of Chiripa. Ceramics from Pukará display similar colors to Paracas wares and incised decoration is common. However, instead of the south coast preference for post-fired painting, Pukará potters decorated their vessels before they were fired. Pukará's power lasted into the first century CE.

THE RISE OF THE LAKESIDE POWERS

On the southeastern shore of the lake, in present-day Bolivia, the site of Tiwanaku began to develop at about the same time as Pukará. Perhaps the two centers were rivals and, if so, Pukará eventually succumbed to the influence of Tiwanaku as it grew into a significant political, economic, and religious power during the Early Intermediate Period.

To the northwest of Lake Titicaca, Chavín influence also apparently never fully took hold of the small local chiefdoms of the Peruvian southern highlands. In the Early Intermediate Period, the Huarpa culture of this region developed a distinct ceramic style that employed red, white, and black slip decoration. This three-color style was taken up and elaborated by the succeeding dominant culture in the area,

PRECEDING PAGES
Lake Titicaca, set amid the vast *altiplano* and majestic mountains.

ABOVE
The round eyes and glaring teeth on this gold Tiwanaku breastplate are distinctively south Andean. The surfaces are left plain to stress the reflective qualities and impressiveness of the material.

OPPOSITE
The Ponce Monolith at Tiwanaku (see pages 110–111) portrays a dignitary with characteristic hat holding ritual feasting objects. Distinctive "tear" motifs descend from the figure's eyes.

known as Wari. Like Tiwanaku, Wari grew to become a great political and cultural power with wide influence in the Andes (see below).

The influences of both Wari and Tiwanaku emanated from two major civic and ritual complexes: the cities of Huari (whence the name of the culture), near modern Ayacucho, and Tiwanaku (sometimes spelled Tiahuanaco). Wari was an expansionist state and Tiwanaku may have had similar ambitions. There appears to have been some kind of frontier in the southern highlands between the two cultures, and their relations may have involved military conflict at various times. An indication that the two powers contested territory and resources can be seen in the Wari fortress of Cerro Baul. It stands atop a huge mesa in the Moquegua River valley, a rich source of minerals that lies in the heart of a Tiwanaku colonial territory.

Whatever the relations between Wari and Tiwanaku, the two states broadly held sway over different regions of the Andes. Wari spread mainly to the north and west, while Tiwanaku influence extended to the far south coast of Peru and through southern Bolivia into northern Chile and Argentina. Huari's location in the Ayacucho

ABOVE
The view from a sunken plaza of the reconstructed portal of the Kalasasaya at Tiwanaku (see page 109). The projecting tenon heads are reminiscent of the New Temple sculptures at Chavín de Huantar, although these Tiwanaku heads show no signs of the effects of hallucinogens and their symbolism is uncertain.

valley presented an easy route to the north through the Mantaro valley but also to the west, via the upper reaches of the coastal river valleys. Huari is quite close to the south coast as well, and both Wari and Tiwanaku cultures appear to have been greatly influenced by the ceramic traditions of that region.

The Inca viewed themselves as having originated in the Titicaca Basin and archaeological research has suggested that they may indeed have inherited many practices from Wari and Tiwanaku. Both cultures of the Middle Horizon therefore appear to lie in a twilight realm, on the edge of historical times but interpreted only through legends, traditions, and the work of archaeologists.

TIWANAKU: CITY OF LEGEND

The ruins of the once great city of Tiwanaku are the stuff of such legends. The huge, abandoned temples and ceremonial precincts captivated the Incas, who saw the place as their ancestral homeland. In 1549 the Spanish conquistador Pedro de Cieza de León visited and described the site, so great was its renown. The American diplomat and

explorer Ephraim George Squier was also struck by the place in the 1870s. The site looms large in the national identity of modern Bolivians. Others have claimed the site as the home of antediluvian lost civilizations and the ruins today attract vast crowds of tourists and seekers of astral knowledge.

By 800CE the vast windswept plain east of Lake Titicaca held a city that covered 2.5 sq miles (6.5 sq km) with as many as 30,000 inhabitants. The site may have been established as early as 100BCE, but it was not until around 300CE that it began to grow from a settlement that may already have covered 0.38 sq miles (1 sq km) in area. Excavations by John W. Janusek have revealed that during Tiwanaku's heyday, commoners lived in residential compounds in a city that was planned around the main monumental ceremonial complexes. Each compound had a large adobe perimeter wall enclosing houses, patios, hearths, storage pits, and trash dumps. Great quantities of food remains have been discovered—quinoa seeds, tubers, maize cobs—together with camelid dung used for fuel and standardized "feasting ware" ceramics. This suggests that the people who lived in such compounds may have participated in accommodating, supplying, and serving the vast number of pilgrims who came to worship at the spectacular ceremonial spaces nearby.

ABOVE
This Tiwanaku vessel, with its handle and bird's head, is made in what is sometimes called the "gravy boat" style. Such distinctive vessels likely held food or liquid for rituals.

MONUMENTAL VISTAS

Tiwanaku underwent continuous remodeling; parts of old structures were reused in new ones. Archaeologists have proposed various theories of how the individual monuments were used, and how they related to one another. Alexi Vranich has suggested that at the city's peak, pilgrims moved through spaces contrived to manipulate their senses, especially vision, to produce feelings of awe.

One part of the ceremonial complex, the Pumapunku, was a combination of a large platform and plaza with a sharply graded approach. On entering the space, visitors would have momentarily lost site of the horizon, only to be confronted by the

RIGHT
The Tiwanaku Sun Gate has impressed visitors for years, partly because it was carved from a single block of stone. The (probably solar) deity and its attendant figures—so-called "angels"—were widespread icons in the Tiwanaku sphere and eventually were adopted by the Wari.

snowcapped Mount Illimani hovering dramatically over the rest of the complex, a half mile away, as they entered the western plaza. A ceremonial space entered later, the Kalasasaya, moved people in the opposite direction, from west to east, away from Illimani and toward Lake Titicaca. Also, while the Pumapunku "opened up" the visitor's perceptions, the Kalasasaya enclosed them. Contained within a raised, rectangular platform 825ft (250m) long, was a sunken court, nearly 500ft (150m) in length, so that pilgrims—perhaps a select few—entered into interior mysteries as they came from outside. Although the sunken court kept those in it from view, it was a far cry from the labyrinths of Chavín.

The largest structure at Tiwanaku, however, was the great Akapana, nearly 857ft long, 650ft wide, and 54ft high (260m by 200m by 16.5m) in the form of a "stepped mountain," a potent Andean symbol since Initial Period times. In its broad top there may have been a deep sunken court or a great hall, while complexes of rooms on either side may have been additional ritual chambers or the residences of priests or nobles. This spectacular monument may have been a symbolic mountain on which the city's priests and rulers represented the great gods. But the messages broadcast from these heights were very different than those of previous times.

OPPOSITE
A hammered and incised Tiwanaku plaque of sheet gold showing a face that was probably once inlaid with stone or shell. The stylized rays around the visage indicate this is the same deity depicted on the Sun Gate at Tiwanaku.

THE GOD OF THE GATEWAY

One of the most impressive and emblematic icons in Andean art is the Gate of the Sun at Tiwanaku (see illustrations on pages 96–97 and 106–107). Above a door-sized entrance in a slab of stone weighing several tons, the carved image of a god is flanked by winged deities running toward him. This "Gateway God" recalls the old Staff God of the Initial Period and the similar being on the Raimondi Stela at Chavín de Huantar (see pages 47–49). Whether he is the same god, whether he presages Viracocha, the supreme deity of the Inca, or whether he represents something else entirely is hard to know. But the imagery itself was already thousands of years old when it was carved.

LEFT
Tiwanaku statuary emphasized solid mass and impressive size. This figure probably represents a lord or anthropomorphic god, wearing the distinctive square hat of authority seen also in the Ponce Monolith (see page 103).

The Gate of the Sun is only one of many monolithic portals at Tiwanaku and the placement of the god above the entryway is significant, linking architectural space and religion in a new way. The three-tiered platform on which he stands has the same plan as the Akapana, suggesting he is the god of the mountains and of Tiwanaku itself. The "staffs" he holds are in fact a spear-thrower, in his right hand, and perhaps darts, in his left. The rays projecting from his head suggest a connection between the deity and the sun, which rises above the mountains to the east; perhaps the darts and spear-thrower are beneficial rays of light.

Even if the weapons refer to war, the god's posture is open, not hostile, suggesting he is at least an ally, if not a friend. The openness is underscored by his placement above the entrance, with winged attendants rushing toward him with their staffs: the pilgrims entering the portal into a sacred precinct would have complemented this scene of adoration as they passed into the holy space.

THE LORD OF HOSPITALITY

When visitors entered the ceremonial spaces of Tiwanaku, they probably saw one or more large stone monoliths in the form of human figures. The largest of these carved monoliths, and indeed the largest in all of South America, stands 24ft (7.3m) tall and is named after Wendell Bennett, one of the first archaeologists to work at Tiwanaku. Another impressive statue is the Ponce Monolith, named after Carlos Ponce, the pioneering Bolivian archaeologist of the site. Both of these statues and other, smaller, examples, depict elaborately clothed figures holding a distinctive ceramic vessel called a *kero* in one

hand and an enigmatic object in the other—a staff, snuff tablet, or perhaps a smaller *kero*. The Inca word *kero* refers to a conically shaped tumbler, often with a flared rim, that was used to drink *chicha*, a beer-like beverage that can be made from many fruits and vegetables but is most often brewed from maize.

Chicha is still the alcoholic beverage of the Andes and is used in ceremonies that often end with the participants in a high state of intoxication. The snakes rising from the *kero* on the Bennett Monolith may indicate the potency of the brew. Among the Inca, drinking was not (and still is not) a solitary activity but always formed part of a social event. The Inca elaborated this practice by often making fancy pairs of *keros*, one of which would be slightly larger than the other. They would be used in ritual drinking to seal alliances between individuals and groups of slightly different status.

BELOW
This Tiwanaku flared drinking cup, or *kero*, from Arama in Bolivia, depicts a feline-headed figure—perhaps a variant of the winged "angel" attendants of the god of the Sun Gate.

OPPOSITE
This *kero* depicts a human face with typical Tiwanaku "tears." It may have been broken as part of the festive rituals in which it was used.

Keros first appear at Tiwanaku and great numbers of them have been found at the site, as well as smashed large beer vessels. That Tiwanaku's most impressive monuments should be statues holding the equivalent of beer glasses is highly significant. We cannot know for certain if these figures are gods or human leaders, but the symbolic offer of hospitality is both literally and figuratively potent.

A CITY OF FESTIVALS

The *keros* and other types of Tiwanaku portable art tend to support the theory that there was a shift in religion away from mystery cults to a style of worship that was more human. Society and the religion that sustained it certainly were hierarchical, however, and there were still many mysteries practiced in religious rites. But the tenor of religion and art seems to have taken a dramatic shift away from esoteric knowledge and practice toward more accessible gods and celebratory rites.The depiction of real people that began in Moche and Recuay art occurs in full force in the Middle Horizon era. Most Tiwanaku portraits were stylized, but all tend to show people clearly recognizable as political leaders, warriors, or priests. Gods, when shown, tend to be much more anthropomorphic than in earlier times.

The open-armed portal gods and the large figures offering *keros* of drink suggest that Tiwanaku's success lay in the development of a new ceremonial complex that was open, welcoming, and festive. Tiwanaku deities and leaders were undoubtedly powerful and commanded respect and awe, but the terrible gods of earlier times appear to have given way to party-givers. Tiwanaku's grand spaces, the movement of people through them to inspire awe and excitement, the staging of elaborate spectacles, and the lubrication of these experiences by plentiful supplies of *chicha*—perhaps laced with hallucinogens—provided a "religious" experience that today could only be reproduced by combining a place of worship, an amusement park, and a beer garden.

HIGHLAND RIVALS

THE WARI EMPIRE

OPPOSITE, TOP AND BOTTOM
Views of Pikillaqta, believed to be a Wari administrative center—its cellular compound architecture made clear by the aerial view. It appears that most of the site was still under construction when it was abandoned.

BELOW
Just over 1in (2.5cm) tall, this Wari figurine combines precious stones, shell, and gold. Forty similar figures were discovered at Pikillaqta.

The Moche may have attempted to develop an expansive state but it appears to have been the Wari who created the first successful Andean empire to endure for a considerable period of time. Many aspects of that success appear to presage the Inca empire, although there is a danger of circular arguments in which the Inca model, known so well, is projected back to Wari, and then Wari is claimed to have laid the foundations of Inca statecraft. Nevertheless, there is substantial evidence to suggest that Wari did indeed hold sway over a great area of what is now Peru.

Wari expanded rapidly in the first epoch of the Middle Horizon (ca. 650CE–1000CE) from its heartland in the Ayacucho valley. Distinctive Wari architectural complexes appeared on the south coast at Cerro Baul, in the southern highlands at Pikillaqta, on the central coast at Pachacamac (see pages 128–131), and in the north highlands at Viracochapampa, among other major sites. Some of these sites clearly were placed in contested territory, such as the hilltop fortification of Cerro Baul in the Moquegua valley, an area colonized by Tiwanaku immigrants. So too, Viracochapampa was constructed in full view of nearby Marcahuamachuco, a massive site with large halls that seems to have been the center of a local confederation. Viracochapampa appears a deliberate imperial challenge to, or replacement of, that older, local system.

Other signs of imperial administration include the first appearance of knotted string recording systems, similar to the later *khipu* of the Inca, and the building of roads, presumably to improve the deployment of armies and the control of population movements from one region to another. Land was reclaimed in some regions and highland populations were relocated to work in fields growing more maize than ever before.

The increased production of maize is intriguing, because maize is nutritionally poorer than many other foods but is preferred for making excellent *chicha* beer. The arrangement of Wari sites and the artifacts found at them suggest that the state sponsored large-scale feasting and drinking festivals. Like the Inca, the Wari may have had a "carrot and stick" approach to expanding their empire: the stick was the imperial

LEFT
The face-neck jar style is typically Wari but the body design is from further afield, to the north. Wari influence in the north coast region has been recognized for years, but scholars still debate if the area succumbed to outright conquest or was more indirectly affected by the empire's might.

ABOVE
The reverse side of a Wari mosaic mirror. The bodiless head with serpents is a shorthand version of the Staff God as seen on the Gateway of the Sun, at Tiwanaku. The image spread widely throughout the region late in the Middle Horizon era.

army and the carrot was the largesse of the empire, expressed in formalized feasting done with distinctive paraphernalia in unique architectural settings.

THE ARCHITECTURE OF EMPIRE

Although Tiwanaku and Wari share many things in common, the architecture of their capital cities is strikingly different. Tiwanaku City is spread across a plain with large plazas, sunken courts, and mounds arranged in rather neat, ordered patterns. Huari, on the other hand, resembles an ancient European city that grew in an unordered, organic fashion over a long period. There appear to have been several great four-sided compounds, surrounded by huge walls that in places still stand more than 33ft (10m) high. Each compound may have been the residence of a noble or aristocrat, but there is no clear relation between one compound and another and the city as a whole sprawls over a rough tableland. The core of the site is about 1 sq mile (2.5 sq km) in area while another 4 sq miles (10 sq km) shows traces of less spectacular architecture.

Huari is so big that it is divided by archaeologists into individual sectors, which have been excavated and studied as separate projects. The apparent disorder of the city is in striking contrast to other, highly structured, Wari centers elsewhere. But, as with ancient Rome, and indeed other European imperial capitals, the city's seemingly unregulated growth may have simply been the result of its age and the original sanctity of a symbolically powerful core area. Rome grew organically from a village or collection of villages centered on a small sacred area; it was already a substantial city before it began imposing strict order in the foreign lands under its domain.

BELOW
The highly stylized abstract geometric design of the turquoise and shell inlay on these ear spools is an example of the shared artistic tastes of Tiwanaku and Wari, making it hard to identify the source of their production with certainty.

A sense of what was occurring at Huari has been achieved through excavations at the contemporary site of Conchopata, a secondary center in the Ayacucho valley. Conchopata recently underwent intensive salvage excavation when it came under threat of severe damage and destruction from the urban development of modern Ayacucho. There, great numbers of large, "face-neck" jars were found. These vessels get their name from the faces painted on their necks, which appear to represent high-ranking individuals. In addition, the bodies of the jars are decorated with elaborate iconography. Great numbers of these vessels were smashed and then ritually buried. However, it is likely that the pots were only "killed" after they had served their purpose of providing copious amounts of *chicha* for the participants in these rites.

Among the most distinctive structures at both Conchopata and Huari are buildings that are shaped rather like a capital letter D, circular in shape apart from a distinct, flat entrance wall. These buildings are large, some almost 65ft (20m) wide at their broadest point, and are commonly lined with niches on the inside. They recall the ancient Kotosh ceremonial chambers (see page 31), although we cannot assume a direct continuity or even a conscious revival, either of the form of the buildings or of the ritual activities which might have taken place within them. While recalling older forms, the architecture is unique, and is another indication of the creative energies of Wari in establishing a new order in the Andes.

The architecture of empire is in evidence at other Wari sites. There are a number of distinctive styles. One includes the use of long, narrow halls with niches in them that are very similar to a later distinctive Inca form known as the *kallanka*. When they were built such structures may have had two or more stories, and would thus have been able to house or entertain many people. One of the most substantial examples is at Viracochapampa, where, according to one theory, the

Wari builders may have deliberately copied the style from the earlier, local center of Marcahuamachuco. It was therefore perhaps an example of the "co-opting" of a local form by an imperial power.

Another possibly later form is cellular architecture consisting of repeated cell-like structures organized on a grid system. One of the largest examples of such cellular architecture is Pikillaqta, the southernmost Wari center (see illustration, page 115). The impressive site, near Cuzco, has huge exterior walls that cut across the rolling landscape as if oblivious to the natural terrain. Almost square in plan, these walls are 4,000ft (1,200m) in length. The largest cell, near the center, covers about 1.85 acres (0.75ha) and was perhaps a courtyard. There are eighteen niched halls in the complex and many smaller, square rooms. To add to this complexity, there may have been additional stories above what remains today, increasing the possible number of activities or residents that Pikillaqta supported.

Many theories have been offered as to the purpose of the small rooms at Pikillaqta and similar sites. It has been proposed that they were barracks or storerooms for the imperial army, ritual chambers, shrines for the bones of revered ancestors, or components of the residence of an imperial governor or other high Wari official. But Pikillaqta is located next to a road, suggesting that it was a power center. This, together with the fact that such complexes may have had upper stories, suggests that it likely served many different imperial purposes.

ABOVE
A Wari camelid fiber hat from the south coast region decorated with stylized human faces and feather headdresses. The four-cornered hat was a distinctive item of clothing for members of the Wari élite (see page 123). The cut pile, similar to thick velvet, was a product of highly skilled and painstaking looping and trimming techniques.

THE MAN IN THE FOUR-CORNERED HAT

To the casual observer or the untrained eye, Wari and Tiwanaku art look identical. Both Wari and Tiwanaku ceramics used brilliant polychromes, usually outlined in black, a tradition they shared with or borrowed from south coast potters. Both art

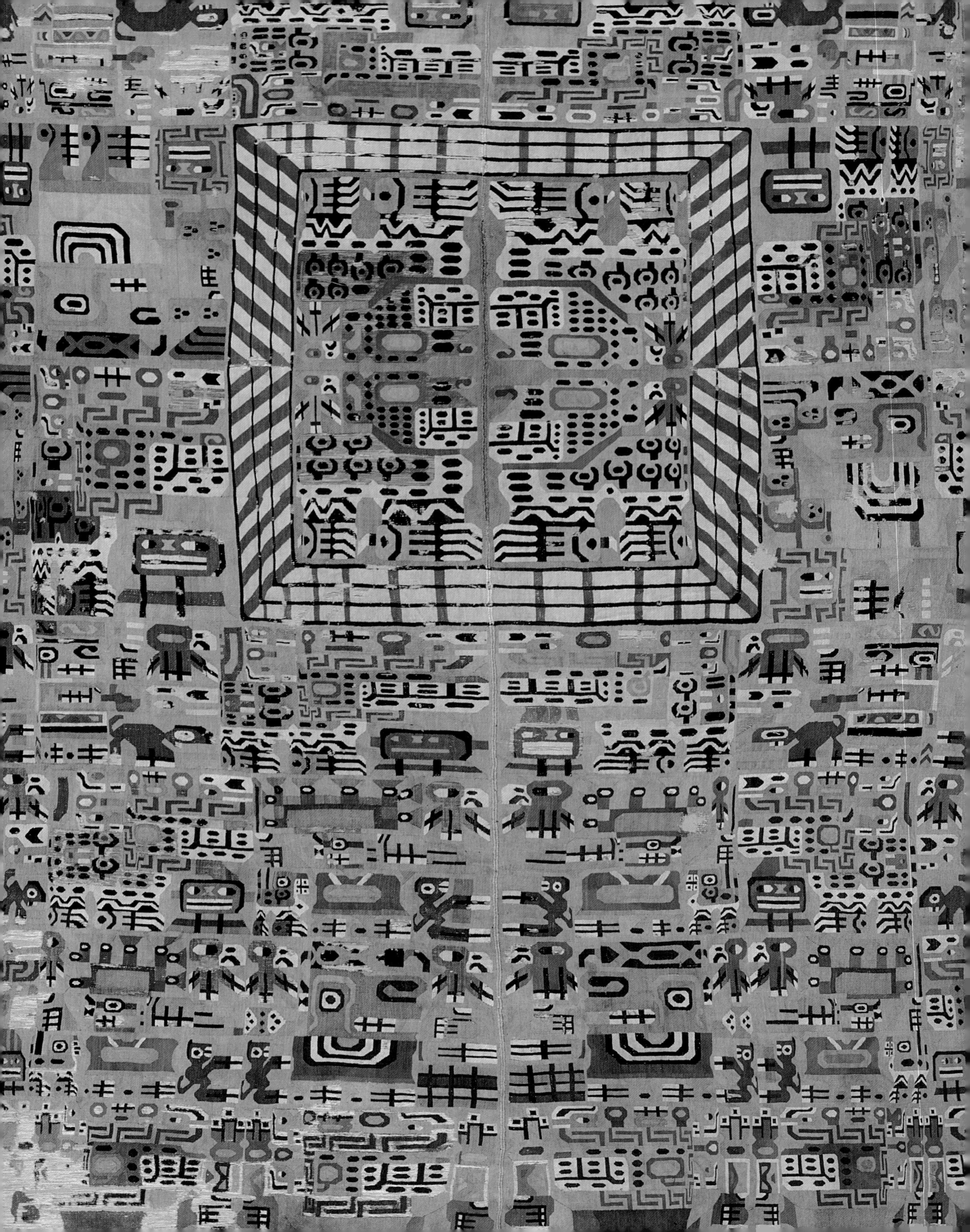

LEFT
A Wari tapestry shirt. The large figures in the two broad stripes appear in highly "condensed" versions on the borders. Most Wari textiles have been found on the coast but it is uncertain whether they were made there or imported from the highlands, and whether styles differed in the two regions.

PRECEDING PAGES
LEFT The "Puma Festival Tunic," a tapestry tunic fragment atypical of Wari style in showing figures that include animals and musicians. The four pumas would have encircled the wearer's neck.
RIGHT The use of tropical bird feathers to produce this cube-shaped hat indicates that it was a special, luxury item.

styles emphasized humans more than deities and the deities that are commonly shown are the Gateway God (see page 109) and his attendants.

However, closer attention reveals significant differences between the two art styles, which are still being discerned. Both art styles may have grown out of the Yaya-Mama tradition, yet Wari may have adopted Tiwanaku religious symbolism late in its history, around 800CE. Why or even how such a transference of symbolism took place is uncertain, because the details of the relationships between the two Andean super-powers are not fully understood. Perhaps this event occurred during a time of peace, perhaps even as a declaration of a joining of forces, such as through a royal marriage, as was common in Europe in the same period when religious conversion was linked to political ties sealed through marriage. Alternatively, Wari could have co-opted its rival's symbolism, claiming to be a more true representative of a universalistic religion than its opponent, again, a pattern seen elsewhere in history more than once. Whether archaeological spade work will ever be able to clarify such fine points of religious and political history is an open question that only time will answer.

One pattern that does emerge from the archaeological record is that both Tiwanaku and Wari were societies with leaders—assisted perhaps by large organized bureaucracies—who oversaw religion, warfare, and feasting. Leaders and bureaucracies were the twin tools of empire. The art styles of both cultures also seem to portray a kind of uniform peculiar to the respective governing élites of Tiwanaku and Wari, and including distinctive tunics and four-cornered hats. The evidence for such costume is clearest for Wari. These hats, together with staffs and *keros*, are emblems of authority that are to be seen on the large polychrome vessels that are so characteristic of the Wari culture.

Four-cornered hats were made of camelid fiber with a looping technique in which additional fibers were inserted into the loops and then trimmed to produce a raised pile. Corner points, sometimes with tassels, were also built up from the panels

ABOVE
A roll-out photograph showing the decoration on an unusual, small Wari *kero*. The human figure wears élite clothing, including the distinctive tall, square hat. He holds the two primary sources of wealth for highland Andean peoples: a stalk of maize, grown at lower altitudes, and a camelid that provided wool and meat, and transported goods.

OPPOSITE
This highly polished polychrome ceramic bottle is typically Wari in style. Winged attendants face each other beneath the image of a grinning skull.

that made the sides of the hat. The designs on the hat consisted of geometric, animal, and bird motifs and, sometimes, running "angels" similar to those on the Gate of the Sun at Tiwanaku (see page 109).

BRILLIANT CLOTHES FOR THE ÉLITE

The tunics of the men who wore the four-cornered hats were among the most spectacular textiles ever produced in the Andes. They were made not on back-strap looms, which were commonly used by Andean weavers, but on large horizontal looms. Whereas Paracas weavers had delighted in embroidery, Wari textile workers used complex tapestry techniques in which the design was literally interwoven into the fabric as a whole. Tiwanaku and Wari tunics are similar in many ways, but Tiwanaku examples tend to more representational forms of decoration while Wari designs become increasingly abstract. In a rare glimpse into the minds of ancient artisans, it is quite clear that true abstraction, in which design elements become ever more stylized, was at work.

Tunics consisted of two separately produced pieces of cloth that were sewn together to make the tunic or shirt. The final product was worn vertically but created horizontally, so that the artisan had to think in two directions simultaneously. The

design elements in the garment, with its long columns of design, consisted of one or two motifs. One common image was a squarish block containing a trophy head and a stepped motif. Such simple elements might be developed into dazzling compositions by alternating different color combinations, by rotating the design, and then repeating patterns of these different combinations within the complete textile. But this was only one of many techniques. Sometimes, the artisan seems to have deliberately broken the pattern, in order to add even more complexity to the piece.

The most startling and fascinating decorative technique of all was the abstraction and compression of a design element so that parts of the figure were wider toward the center of a tunic but abbreviated into a few simple elements near the edge. To a viewer not fully aware of the technique, this would have presented a bewildering combination of order and disorder at the same time. Many examples of this technique survive but it is uncommon to find it repeated in exactly the same manner on more than one kind of tunic. This suggests that while these distinctive tunics were indeed made for high-status individuals, they were less of a literal uniform than a restricted style, perhaps created in accordance with a set of official guidelines.

According to one estimate, the finest tunics contained somewhere between 6 to 9 miles (10–14km) of camelid thread. This fact, combined with the labor that went into weaving and dying the fabrics, indicates that these articles of clothing were clearly produced for a very small, élite segment of society. Perhaps the leaders of Wari society were not bureaucrats after all but aristocrats, leaders of

OPPOSITE
A detail of a feather mantle showing two eight-pointed stars and a two-headed feline-serpent. While not unique to Wari, the two-headed creature was particularly popular, while the star, perhaps referring to both dualism and the four directions, found special favor in the southern highlands and coast.

clans or communities, each competing with the others to commission, within fairly strict rules, the most spectacular and distinctive tunic.

WINDS OF CHANGE

The southern highland cultures had risen when Moche was in trouble. While these changes were taking place there was a great drought lasting from 562 to 594CE, probably tied to El Niño events. Contrary to the view that the imperial expansion of Tiwanaku and Wari was strictly militaristic in nature, there is a theory that the success of the highland cultures was mostly due to innovative agricultural techniques that may have helped them not only to weather the drought but also to prosper.

According to this theory, Tiwanaku spread across the *altiplano* by developing irrigated, ridged fields (irrigation agriculture may have been practiced in the Andes in the later part of the Preceramic Period), thereby extending the growing season and producing more aerated and fertile soils. Tiwanaku also developed long-distance caravans, colonies, and outposts. Wari built irrigation canals that tapped high altitude water sources and connected to systems that watered extensive terraces. Wari administrative centers, such as Pikillaqta, would have further helped to organize and rationalize labor and resources in areas into which they expanded.

Between around 800CE and 1000CE unsettled times returned, and on this occasion they came to the empires of the highlands. Ridged field systems collapsed and agricultural terraces dried up. Once again, environmental factors were at work, but whether they were the predominant cause of the end of the Middle Horizon states or one of several contributing factors is hard to ascertain. As Tiwanaku and Wari declined, the world of the central Andes relapsed into a period of regional states. However, while there were times of political instability, population densities appear to have remained high enough in some regions for centralized political authorities to reformulate themselves fairly quickly.

PACHACAMAC: THE CITY OF THE ORACLE

When Francisco Pizarro captured the Inca emperor Atahualpa, he quickly learned of the sacred Inca capital city of Cuzco and also of another holy city called Pachacamac. Continuing a tradition that stretched back through Tiwanaku and Wari times to Chavín and beyond, Pachacamac was the home of a powerful oracle worshipped throughout Peru. So important were the shrine and its city that Pizarro quickly dispatched his brother, Hernando, to ride down the coast with his men and seize the site.

Pachacamac, near modern Lima, sits at the edge of the sea near the mouth of the Lurín River valley with a huge sand dune to its north. Traces suggest that this place was first occupied in the Preceramic Period, but the site rose to prominence in about 300–400CE, in the Early Intermediate Period, when it became a cult and pilgrimage center of the Lima culture (see pages 93–94). The architectural core of the complex is 0.4 sq mile (1 sq km) in area, with additional streets and structures beyond it. At the far western end, overlooking the sea, is the massive "Temple of the Sun," 654ft (200m) wide at its base and 12 acres (4.85ha) in area. It towers above the rest of the city on a hill that makes it seem much higher than the 65ft (20m) or so of actual structure.

Nearby stood a temple that was even more important than the massive sun temple. It contained the idol of Pachacamac himself, the deity that was the focus of the pilgrims' journeys and adoration, the "creator and sustainer of the universe" in the words of an early chronicler, and the lord of earthquakes. Precisely how the oracle functioned is not known; perhaps Pachacamac "spoke" through a priest. Over the centuries two successive temples were constructed on the site.

On the northern and western side of the oracle temple stood some distinctive architectural complexes known as "Pyramids with Ramps." Built and rebuilt with slight variations, at least fifteen times, one such complex was close to 327ft (100m) in length and half that in width, and included a courtyard with a ramp that led into suites of rooms with interior passages and patios. These rooms include domestic quarters, storage areas, and halls, probably for receiving visitors and performing ceremonies.

RIGHT, ABOVE
The "Pyramid with Ramp" at the Pachacamac complex. Built of adobe bricks and once brightly painted, this would have been an imposing structure. Ceremonies would have been impressive, as dignitaries ascended and descended the ramps, which were an especially coastal form of architecture.

RIGHT, BELOW
A pair of Wari-influenced drinking vessels decorated as skulls that are said to have come from Pachacamac, indicating Wari influence at the site. The vessels are almost identical but slightly unequal in size. This suggests that drinking rituals emphasizing asymmetrical dualism, which are known for the Inca, were also practiced by their Wari predecessors.

ABOVE

Once painted bright red, the Inca Sun Temple at Pachacamac commanded a view of the mouth of the Lurín valley and its fields as well as of the Pacific Ocean, both sources of sustenance and wealth. According to myth, the offshore islands were once ancestor-heroes who were said to have been transformed.

A PALACE FOR THE GUARDIANS OF THE ORACLE?

One theory is that the sets of rooms were the "religious embassies" of distant Andean communities who wanted a permanent representation at the great religious center. Alternative theories suggest that each "Pyramid with Ramp" was the palace of a ruler of Pachacamac, or that the complexes were the residences of a series of rulers within a single dynasty. There is evidence for more than one elaborate burial in the compounds, unfortunately usually looted. There is also evidence that these complexes were ritually "buried" by being covered with soil and adobe bricks, perhaps when one dynasty ended and a new one began, each building its own, new complex elsewhere.

Whatever the specific purposes of the pyramids, it is clear that Pachacamac was a holy site visited by people from throughout Peru. Recently, archaeologists Izumi Shimada and Rafael Segura excavated in what has been called the "Plaza of the Pilgrims," in front of the more recent of the two temples of Pachacamac. They discovered layer upon layer of a bewildering variety of offerings, more than 3ft (1m) deep. They included whole fish and maize left exposed on floors and carefully placed

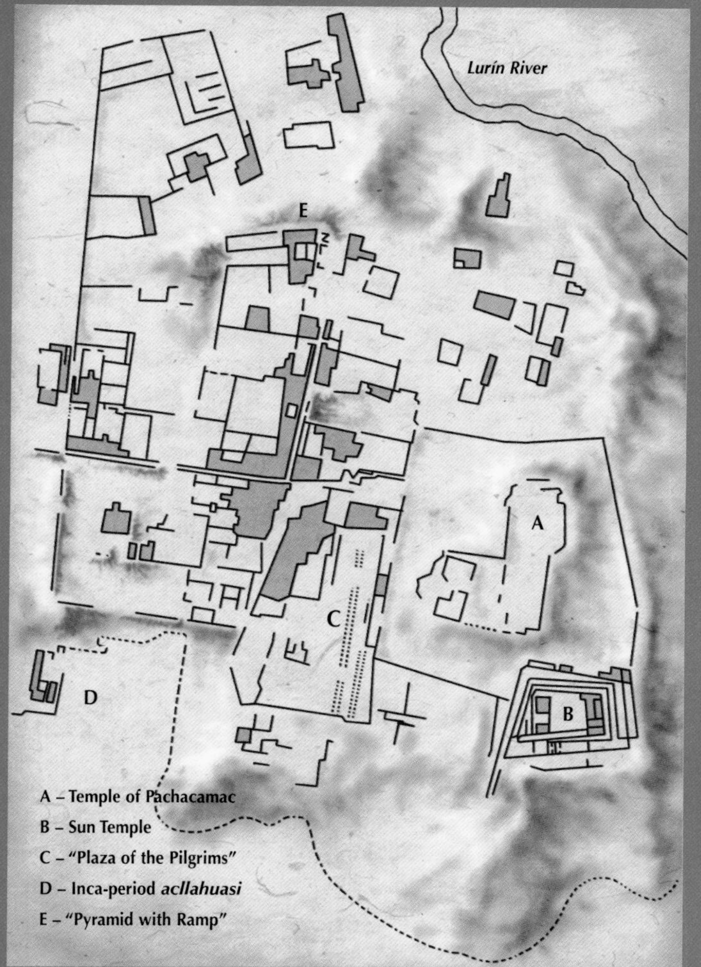

LEFT
Established on a hilly site between the Lurín River and the sea, the religious complex at Pachacamac consisted of a variety of structures (see key), but the most important were the Temple of Pachacamac (A) and the Sun Temple (B).

clusters of field stones and broken shards that challenge the traditional notion of ritual offerings. The positions of these offerings related to large and small jars that had been placed inside carefully built adobe or stone enclosures. The excavators suspect that these vessels represented venerated ancestors.

Pachacamac became such an important shrine that it appears that each succeeding Andean empire tried to co-opt it, rather than conquer it. The Wari built extensively at the site and a distinct emblem, known as the "Pachacamac Griffin" seems to have been associated with their presence at the complex. Later, the Inca built the massive Sun Temple.

SACRIFICES FOR THE WOODEN IDOL

But the focus of the city, and the most important shrine throughout its history, was the Temple of Pachacamac. This is the deity's Inca name, but it was probably an ancient god, stretching back to time immemorial. His relationship with the two other important deities venerated at the site, called Pachamama (Earth Mother) and Mamacocha (Mother Sea) by the Incas, is uncertain. But the location of his principal shrine directly next to the sea—Mamacocha herself—is probably significant.

When the Spanish desecrated the inner sanctum of Pachacamac's shrine they did not find the golden idol and the treasures they expected. Instead, all they found was a simple wooden idol in human form, in a room caked in the blood of innumerable sacrifices. Near the site of the shrine archaeologists discovered a carved wooden idol on a pole, but whether this is a representation of the same god, a replica, or some other deity is unknown. The original image was destroyed, to the shock of its devotees.

chapter 5

KINGDOMS OF GOLD

THE LATE INTERMEDIATE PERIOD

CA. 1000CE–CA. 1450CE

LEFT

A gold Chimú funerary mask, still bearing traces of red (cinnabar) paint—as well as the unmistakeable stylistic influence of Lambayeque, whose artisans came under Chimú rule as the kingdom of Chimor expanded into the Lambayeque valley.

EMPIRES UNDONE, EMPIRES EMERGING

A HOST OF STATES AND KINGDOMS

BELOW
Spectacular wooden coffins, each containing a mummy, stand in the cliffs at Karajia as a reminder of the Chachapoyas, or Cloud Forest people. They dominated this mountainous tropical jungle terrain from monumental ridgetop citadels, until the rise of the Inca led to their subjugation and dispersal.

The demise of the great highland powers of Tiwanaku and Wari was followed by a time of troubles and instability, and numerous regional states and kingdoms eventually emerged in their wake in the Late Intermediate Period (ca. 1000–1450CE). In the central highlands, near the modern city of Jauja, the Wanka consisted of weakly linked communities, alternately fighting and allying with one another. Fortified Wanka settlements, large and small, were spread across the upper Yanamarca River valley. Similarly, around Lake Titicaca, the Lupaca kingdom eventually rose to preeminence within a complex political landscape, building its wealth on great camelid herds and, probably, military might. The coastal region experienced the same pattern of small political units in some areas and larger, expansionist ones elsewhere.

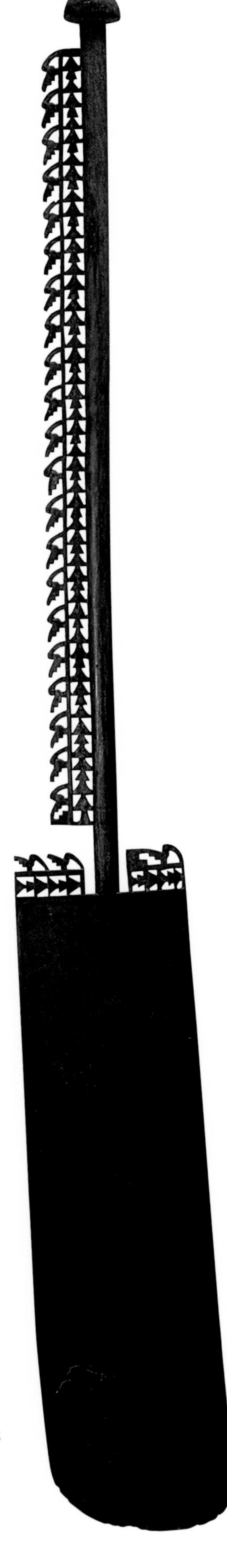

RIGHT
Painted wooden objects such as this one, possibly Ica or Chincha, are among the most enigmatic of ancient Peru. They have been interpreted as ceremonial digging sticks, as paddles, and as steering boards for rafts.

The succeeding Inca empire was of short duration in many parts of the Andes and so a rich oral tradition of life before the Inca and Spanish conquests is available for many areas. These tales, combined with archaeology, help to present a picture of a complex world of ceremonial centers, cities, shrines, and trading centers in western South America. For example, the great pilgrimage center of Pachacamac continued to be open to all, but after the waning of Wari imperial might the site came under the control of the Ichma, when numerous "Pyramids with Ramps" were built. Farther north, the Moche state or states had been shaken by natural disasters (see page 94). Recent research suggests that Wari influences gained a foothold in the region soon after. The embracing of new symbolic forms combined with population movements, the abandonment of some sites, and the growth of others eventually led to the end of Moche and the establishment of a new order on the north coast of Peru.

Some of the changes occurred gradually, others dramatically. As new political and economic powers emerged there was a marked increase in the production of ceramics, textiles, and other goods and an accompanying increase in trade, local and distant. All these factors indicate that the world of the late prehistoric Andes was an increasingly multicultural one.

NEW ARTS FOR NEW MESSAGES

Beginning with Recuay (see pages 92–93) and continuing through Wari and Tiwanaku, there was a trend in art toward decreasing emphasis on mythology and increasing emphasis on the world of humans. This trend came even more to the fore in the cultures of the Late Intermediate Period. While many societies of this period still appear to have deified their rulers, much of their art appears to have been produced for a wider market than solely the élite.

In general, pottery production was simplified. On the central and northern coasts, artists commonly used two-piece molds to produce multiple copies of the

RIGHT
The Chancay culture of the central coast produced vivid textiles and simple black-and-white ceramics. This (female) effigy jar figurine depicts a supernatural deity known as *chuchimilco* and was one of a pair, male and female, made as a tomb offering.

ABOVE
Ceramic vessels in the form of buildings, such as this small Lambayeque representation of a temple or palace, offer an insight into ancient architecture. While many buildings remain standing, details of architectural decoration are often missing. Note the two small figures of guards at what must have been an important palace or temple.

same design. Decoration was kept simple, in many cases using just one or two colors. Lambayeque (Sicán) and Chimú ceramics were mostly black. Those of Ica and Chincha usually had a single decorative band running around the vessel.

Artists of the Chancay culture of the central coast often used black paint on white-slipped ceramics. Many pots are decorated in a rather slapdash manner with simple, geometric designs, and frequent drip marks on the vessel suggest that artisans were working in a hurry. In contrast to their ceramics, however, Chancay textiles were brilliantly colorful. Figures (sometimes erroneously referred to as "dolls") were made depicting the costumes of women at the loom, other people, llamas, and "trees of life." They are charming to modern tastes but they, like pairs of ceramic male and female figurines, were probably all made for a growing mortuary industry. The Chancay repertoire additionally includes quickly produced, freestyle painted textiles that also appeal to modern tastes and inspired Paul Klee and other modern artists. However, these textiles also point to a new kind of society in which many more people acquired fancy grave goods for burial with their dead.

Elsewhere, textiles continued to be technologically complex and beautiful but often their designs were repetitive, consisting of geometric motifs or simple renditions of fish, birds, felines, and the like. Such designs can be traced all the way back to Huaca Prieta (see page 25) and it is as if the simple appreciation of design had reasserted itself in Andean art. While it is always tempting to interpret even simple images as laden with symbolism, the overall impression of Late Intermediate Period art is that it was more decorative than symbolic. There appears to have been a shift away from producing objects out of precious substances in order to convey meaning,

RIGHT

Chancay figures, more popularly misnamed "dolls," were made of wrapped yarn and embroidered textiles. Also intended for tomb offerings, the figures' recent popularity with collectors has resulted in the severe looting of sites and the production of many fakes.

OPPOSITE

The painted figures on this Chancay cloth may appear whimsical to us but it is reasonable to suppose that they possessed symbolic power for the artist who created them. Painted textiles, popular in the Early Horizon era, regained their popularity in the Late Intermediate Period. Painting may have helped to speed production, a process also seen in ceramics.

toward producing objects whose meaning was that they were valuable. It is easy to imagine that large textiles with repeating patterns in bright colors were designed as wall hangings to express the power and wealth of high-ranking nobles, rather than to convey specific meanings about relationships between humans and the divine.

DRESSING TO IMPRESS

The trend towards less intensely symbolic art also can be seen in the costumes and regalia of rulers and priests. In earlier times, many high-status goods were delicately wrought, such as Moche ear spools with their finely detailed designs. Careful artisanship can only be appreciated from a short distance so, presumably, such fine jewelry was meant to impress competing rulers or a small retinue of aristocrats, gathered in a council chamber. By contrast, the costume of Late Intermediate potentates aims to dazzle from afar. Broad surfaces of sheet metal were composed to form headdresses. Shirts were adorned with little metal bangles that would have shimmered in the sunlight across a grand plaza. Even drinking vessels were made in "super-size" dimensions

LEFT
A Chancay burial "mask" painted red with inlaid eyes. These simple wooden masks were a feature of the art of the Late Intermediate Period. Their stark, dramatic imagery may indicate a more widespread development of ancestor cults beyond the élites.

so that, perhaps, a ceremony of libations (liquid offerings) could be seen by a large crowd who would not discern the details but would be impressed by the consequent glitter and razzle-dazzle.

As with most cultural patterns in Andean prehistory, these trends began earlier, during the Middle Horizon. However, in the Late Intermediate Period, Andean cults surrounding the dead took on new meanings. It may be that once state sponsorship of such feasting of ancestors waned, with the collapse of the highland empires, local people reclaimed their right to remember their own ancestors in their own ways. In doing so they perhaps drew upon ancient ideas, reinterpreted Middle Horizon concepts, and created new ones. One of those new ideas appear to be *chullpa*s, aboveground burial structures, often in the shape of square or round towers, which were particularly popular in the old area of Wari and Tiwanaku.

OPPOSITE
A *chullpa*, or stone burial tower, at Sillustani near Puno. *Chullpa*s became common in the Late Intermediate Period and indicate an increased emphasis on ancestor cults. Individual *chullpa*s proclaimed the importance of particular kinship groups and at the same time gave descendants easy access to the mummies of their honored dead, in order to "feed" and perhaps consult them.

NAYMLAP'S REALM

THE GOLD OF LAMBAYEQUE

OPPOSITE
This detail of a Lambayeque pectoral cut from sheet gold depicts a stylized figure whose distinctive double-tasseled belt is reminiscent of Moche mythic heroes, suggesting a continuation of that symbolism into later times. Sheet metal grew in popularity in the Late Intermediate Period. Its use made it easier to cover large areas, whether of walls or costumes, that would reflect the sunlight. The resulting brilliant effect was probably intended to impress the enormous crowds that characterized the cults of the time.

Out of the mists where Andean legend and history blur together comes a story, recorded in 1586. In ancient times, a fleet of balsa rafts sailed towards the Lambayeque River valley, bringing a king called Naymlap and his retinue: Pitz Zofi, Preparer of the Way; Fonga Sigde, Blower of the Shell Trumpet; Ninacola, Master of the Litter and Throne; Ninagintue, Royal Cellarer; Llapchillulli, Purveyor of Feathercloth Garments; Xam Muchec, Steward of the Facepaint; Occhocalo, Royal Cook; and Ollopcopoc, Master of the Bath. Naymlap brought with him a greenstone idol called Yampellec, from which the Lambayeque valley took its name. The king established a dynasty but it eventually fell to the empire of the Chimú, coming from the south to conquer it.

It is not known how historically accurate this tale may be. But the legend provides a rich source of material for imagining what the royal court of Lambayeque (also called Sicán) must have been like. The titles of those in the royal entourage reflect the things to which great importance was attached, such as feathercloth clothing, in which brilliant tropical bird feathers were individually knotted to a woven textile to create a shimmering mantle or cloak. Shell trumpets are known from the Initial Period and it is interesting that an officer of the court may have been granted a title that referred to them. So too, Fonga Sigde, Preparer of the Way, was said to have scattered shell dust wherever his lord was about to walk. This was probably spondylus shell dust and underscores the importance of the shell in late Andean prehistory and the great quantities that were consumed at that time (see pages 150–153 and 159–160).

As the Moche collapsed in its southern valleys, there seems to have been a reorganization and reestablishment of the northern Moche, including the rise to prominence of the huge city of Pampa Grande. But it, too, eventually succumbed. The succeeding Lambayeque culture may have consisted of separate centers, all loosely affiliated by ties to mythical or real ancestors such as Naymlap. The pyramids of Batán Grande comprise one of the greatest such centers, with a civic core that alone covers

RIGHT
A Lambayeque burial mask cut from sheet gold with inlaid copper used for the classic "comma-shaped" Lambayeque eyes and the nose ornament. Produced for a king or important noble, it may represent the figure known as the Sicán Lord. Masks such as this are among the most emblematic images of ancient Peru. One theory proposes that the mask may have been intended to transform the wearer into a god in the afterlife.

LEFT
Another emblematic Andean object is this Lamabyeque *tumi* (semicircular knife) in gold and precious stones. The figure wears a "Sicán Lord" god-mask like the one on the previous pages—or perhaps this is the god himself, whose image was copied in burial masks for the élite dead.

1.5 sq miles (4 sq km) containing more than a dozen pyramids. Research by Izumi Shimada and colleagues there suggests that it was an important religious center, perhaps similar to the southern oracle city of Pachacamac (see pages 128–131).

RICHES FOR THE LORDS OF LAMBAYEQUE

The Lambayeque culture took metalworking to new heights, and in the many Lambayeque workshops technical innovations were matched by organizational ones emphasizing mass production and efficiency. Large, flat masks of precious metal, with distinctive "comma-shaped" eyes, characterize Lambayeque high-status burials, with some masks elaborately augmented by paint and other metalwork, including bangles, nose ornaments, and ray-like objects projecting from the eyes (see pages 144–145, for example). Large silver or gold *keros* were also a distinctive feature of the culture and among looters' tales are reports of more than 150 such items being found in one tomb. At the other extreme, excavators have discovered substantial quantities of small I-shaped copper bars, or *naipes*, at Batán Grande. Also found in Ecuador and Mexico, *naipes* may have served as a kind of international proto-money for the burgeoning trading systems along the Pacific coast.

While metalworking continued to expand in terms of the availability, technology, and diversity of forms, the role of ceramics may have diminished. New vessel shapes occur, however, and the spout-and-bridge of the south coast makes an appearance, perhaps due to increased contacts along the coast. Unlike the southern form, Lambayeque vessels often include a pedestal base, a detail more popular in Ecuador and farther north, suggesting another source of influence—again probably owing to increased maritime contacts. A predominant image on these plain black or gray vessels is a

figure known as the "Sicán Lord." This individual is usually shown only from the neck up, often with elaborate ear spools and a conical hat, formed by the spout. He has a beak-like nose and sometimes sports talons instead of feet, while small wings are sometimes depicted on his shoulders. The Sicán Lord may be a depiction of Naymlap, the legendary founder of the mighty Lambayeque kingdom. The myth of Naymlap ends with his death, but before his demise he commanded his aides to tell the people that he has grown wings and flown away.

ABOVE
The striking facial features of this Lambayeque copper mask almost suggest portraiture, but more likely denote a stylized mythic personality. Light reflecting off the accompanying mother-of-pearl necklace would have made an impressive display.

LEFT

Sumptuous golden Lambayeque *keros* such as these were used in drinking rituals. The repeating pattern of the Sicán Lord on one vessel (far left) and the turquoise inlays on the others exemplify the preference for luxury items that display a relatively low level of symbolism but are fashioned from materials of great value.

THE QUEST FOR THE THORNY OYSTER: LONG-DISTANCE TRADE

In 1513 Vasco Nuñez de Balboa, stumbling through the jungles of Panama, glimpsed a distant shimmer through the trees. Shortly afterward he became the first European to gaze upon the Pacific Ocean. More than half a century later, the Spanish court chronicler claimed that a chief named Tumaco told Balboa that the Pacific coast continued over a great distance, "without end," and that much farther along it was a land where there was much gold. Tumaco molded from earth one of the strange beasts that people in those distant lands used to carry burdens.

This account is the only record of the meeting of Balboa and Tumaco and was written several decades after the Spanish had conquered Peru. Understandably, perhaps, scholars have cast doubt on the story's authenticity and have tended to assume that it was fabricated for some political motive. How could a chief in Panama have known of the riches of Peru, thousands of miles to the south?

Discoveries in the last few years have perhaps lent more credence to the tale. There is now convincing evidence that between around 600CE and 1300CE specialized metalworking techniques were introduced to western Mexico from the south. Lost-wax casting came from Central America or Colombia, while cold working arrived from southern Ecuador or northern Peru. There are enough intervening areas where these technologies are not found to suggest that they traveled to Mexico not overland but by sea. Furthermore, distinctive ceramic styles and "boot-shaped" tombs are found, among other things, in both western Mexico and areas near the modern Ecuador–Peru frontier. This suggests that more was exchanged between the two regions than metalworking techniques.

At the time of the Spanish conquest, Andean peoples had sufficient memories of life before the Inca to give us a very clear picture

BELOW
After the spines had been removed from this *Spondylus princeps* shell it was polished and inlaid with purple *Spondylus calcifer,* darker *Spondylus princeps,* and turquoise. The bird pecking at a fish is a common Chimú motif that expresses the natural order of predator and prey.

LEFT
This blackware Chimú vessel underscores the importance of the thorny oyster for the Chimú. The figure holds an exceptionally large *Spondylus princeps*. As provider or owner of the shell, such a person was worthy of respect and perhaps even awe.

of a busy maritime highway along the Pacific shoreline in the Late Intermediate Period. Such travel also probably occurred much earlier, but by late prehistory the seas were plied by huge, long-distance trading vessels. There may have been many coastal Ecuadorian and Peruvian communities specializing in long-distance trade. The Manteño culture in Ecuador was probably one such community, while the people of La Puna, a large island in the Gulf of Guayaquil, have been called the "Vikings of the Pacific" for the stories told of their seafaring adventures—La Puna voyages typically combined trading and opportunistic raiding.

On Peru's south coast, 124 miles (200km) south of Lima, stands La Centinela, a large adobe ruin near the mouth of the Chincha River valley. Research has identified the rulers of this citadel and valley as masters of overseas trade. The Chincha were so successful at traveling far to the north that when the Inca conquered them they erected just one building at La Centinela (probably for the Inca administrator), but otherwise allowed the Chincha to carry on their trading activities unhindered. All the Inca demanded was a portion of the profits of a successful enterprise in which several thousand people were reported to be engaged.

RED TREASURE FROM THE SEA

What was so precious that coastal dwellers ventured far from home for many months? Dark blue lapis lazuli was prized and brought from Chile, while colorful tropical bird feathers were sought deep in the distant tropical forests. But one prize was desired above all: spondylus. This beautiful oyster with spikes rising from its bright red shell

LEFT
A large frontal of an earspool showing men and spondylus shells. The design appears to celebrate the distribution of the thorny oyster, although no actual shell is used in this ornament. However, two other prized materials, blue stone and gold, made it an object of value.

is found only in the warm tropical waters of Ecuador and farther north. A larger, smoother, variety of spondylus was prized for its purple shell and used for inlays and other decorations, but the red *Spondylus princeps* was thought to be the very food of the gods and is an essential ingredient, even today, for many traditional rituals. Spondylus is found in deep waters and required divers with special skills to hold their breath for long periods and chase after the shellfish that could move about in the depths to avoid predators.

LEFT, ABOVE
Expeditions for spondylus required large balsa rafts, but fishermen on the coast and on Lake Titicaca generally used reed boats like these. They are still made today in both areas; it takes eight months for the reeds to become waterlogged and the same amount of time to make a new one, so that boats are always being produced.

LEFT, BELOW
The Inca referred to spondylus shells as *chaquira* and prized them most highly. But other shells, such as the ones used to make these necklaces, were also desirable, if perhaps less so.

Traces of spondylus shell are found at Preceramic sites, more remains are found at Initial Period centers, and after that spondylus is present at archaeological sites in ever increasing numbers through to the end of Andean prehistory. By the Late Intermediate Period, spondylus was being imported into Peru in vast quantities and Peruvian traders probably voyaged farther north, perhaps even as far as Mexico, to supply an ever-growing demand for the shell in their homelands (see pages 159–160).

In 1527, while investigating the regions he was soon to conquer, Francisco Pizarro encountered a large raft made of huge logs, estimated to weigh about thirty tons. Pizarro's pilot, Bartolomé Ruiz, stated that it had a mast and sail of cotton and was manned by a crew of twenty. The raft carried many pieces of silver and gold, in the form of ornaments and decorations, as well as rich and elaborate textiles and garments of both cotton and wool. All of this wealth was brought in order to get "some seashells from which they make colored beads of coral color and white." There can be little doubt that this was a spondylus trader—one of the last in a busy commercial enterprise that had begun hundreds of years before but rocketed to importance in the Late Intermediate Period.

THE EMPIRE OF CHIMOR

MIGHTY RIVALS OF THE INCA

OPPOSITE, ABOVE
Friezes featuring repetitious images of these curious squirrel-like animals—possibly nutria or coypu—adorn long stretches of the walls of Chan Chan. The enormous site has been identified as the ancient city of Chimor, capital of the Chimor (now known as Chimú) kingdom.

OPPOSITE, BELOW
The so-called Temple of the Rainbow at Chan Chan is decorated, like many of the sprawling city's structures, with striking adobe reliefs displaying animal and geometric motifs. The design of this panel is particularly complex.

Standing even brighter than Lambayeque in the reflected light of historic times is the great empire known today as Chimú. Owing to the accounts given by old people at the time of the Spanish arrival in Peru, we know that the kingdom and its capital were in fact called Chimor and that Chimú was the title of its ruler. An origin legend similar to that of the Lambayeque, whom Chimor conquered, also persisted long enough to be recorded in colonial times. It tells of a founder named Taycanamu and a dynasty of rulers down to King Minchançaman, who surrendered to the Inca. There were nine to eleven monarchs in the dynasty, depending on how the records are interpreted. The question of the number of rulers is important, because it may or may not relate directly to archaeological remains.

There is no doubt that Chimor, the capital of the Chimor kingdom, was the site now known as Chan Chan, on the northern side of the Moche River valley, today only a few minutes drive from the Moche *huaca*s where their ancestors had lived. The site is huge, covering 7.7 sq miles (20 sq km) of the valley mouth, directly on the shore. Within this vast city there were residential areas for 26,000 commoners, most of whom were likely devoted to producing textiles, metalwork, and ceramics. The Chimú ruling class may have numbered about six thousand, living in large brick enclosures, while many thousands of servants lived close to the quarters of their masters. No farmers or fisherman dwelt in the city, as it was exclusively designed as a place of governance, crafts, and commerce. Society was highly stratified—one Chimú legend stated that each class was born of a separate egg: a gold egg for noblemen, silver for noblewomen, and copper for commoners.

PALACES OF THE LIVING AND THE DEAD

Within the sprawling metropolis there was an area of great enclosures called *ciudadelas* (citadels) by the Spanish and covering 2.3 sq miles (6 sq km). Depending on how they are counted, there are as many as ten of these compounds, which some scholars

BELOW
A general view of the mile upon mile of adobe compound walls that constitute the impressive remains at Chan Chan. One of the characteristics of Chimú art at Chan Chan is its limited range of decorative motifs replicated systematically—not dissimilar in fact to textile patterning.

RIGHT
A detail of warriors and mythological creatures among the carved adobe images adorning Chan Chan's Temple of the Rainbow.

ABOVE
The impressive citadel of Paramonga overlooks the lower Fortaleza River valley. It is considered by many to have been a Chimú fortress at the southern limits of their empire. The massive adobe brick structure rises in tiers to dominate the surrounding area, and in places its walls bear evidence of plaster and colorful paint. The structures on top have stone floors and distinctive trapezoidal doorways.

have tried to tie to the list of kings in the Chimú origin legend. Other scholars have noted that the architectural styles of the *ciudadelas* are such that they may have been built in pairs, suggesting a form of dual leadership that was common for Andean political systems (see page 174). The architecture of the enclosures changed over time and some of them have been severely looted, but there is a general pattern to their design that suggests that these were indeed the residences, and probably also the mausoleums, of the great kings of Chimor.

The most elaborate *ciudadelas* were designed to impress. Following trends that were centuries old, their builders put less emphasis on height than on vast spaces, spread out in a huge horizontal layout within high perimeter walls and including large walk-in wells. Some of the compounds required the visitor to walk down long passageways and double back before entering an open space—reminiscent of the labyrinths of Chavín de Huantar (see Chapter 2) but now with a secular purpose.

Relatively small rooms, known in Spanish as *audiencias* (audience chambers), were likely the residences of royal administrators within the compounds. Again recall-

RIGHT
A Chimú ceremonial *kero* made of wood inlaid with gold and turquoise and showing the figure of a man. It illustrates the Chimú propensity for highly decorative artworks.

ing ancient patterns, the *audiencia* often consisted principally of a U-shaped adobe chamber with niches in its walls. In the spaces surrounding the *audiencia* were other chambers and raised square receptacles, which have been interpreted as storage spaces for luxury goods, perhaps spondylus, metal, and textiles. These may have been for tribute brought to the king, or for gifts presented to visitors as signs of the king's hospitality and largesse.

Farther back in the *ciudadela* and probably off-limits to all but the most important or intimate acquaintances of the king, were residential areas. Finally, in the back was a mortuary complex, consisting of a large central chamber surrounded by many smaller cell-like crypts. From the reports of conquistadors and the investigations of modern archaeologists, it is fairly certain that the large chamber was the burial place of a ruler while the smaller cells were filled with offerings—including sacrificed women—for the king's afterlife.

The Chimú supposedly took Lambayeque smiths as prisoners, forcing them to work at Chan Chan. Later, the Inca did the same when they conquered the Chimú, making their best artisans leave to work in Cuzco. It was the Inca who first looted many of Chan Chan's burial chambers, to be followed several decades later by the Spanish. Some scholars have suggested that the Inca took a lot more than just plunder from Chan Chan. For example, the idea of a monarch continuing to reside in his palace after death, with his family maintaining his royal estate and controlling his property, was perhaps a Chimú concept adopted by the Inca as they expanded into an empire.

THE ART OF CHIMÚ

If Lambayeque was developing an expertise in long-distance trade, the Chimú conquest of Lambayeque was perhaps motivated by a desire to monopolize the business. Spondylus is a constant, repeated image in Chimú art. The shell is used in

RIGHT
A beaten golden plaque, probably originally sewn to a textile. The body of the central figure has been reduced to a squat trunk and two small feet. The flanking creatures may be variants of the "Moon Animal," seen in Recuay and Moche art.

a wide variety of inlays and ornaments. Perhaps more significantly, as an indication of the preoccupation with spondylus that seems to have developed in this period (see pages 150–153), depictions of the shell itself are ubiquitous. Men are shown holding the shell as if showing off their finds. A series of silver plates depict various people and, perhaps, deities in pursuit of spondylus. Spondylus fishermen, diving from rafts after the precious shell, complete with safety lines around them, are even depicted on an adobe frieze in one of the *ciudadelas* at Chan Chan.

ABOVE
These elaborate Chimú *keros* are each made of a single sheet of silver and were probably buried with a nobleman. Although gold was the more precious metal, silver objects are rarer than gold ones because silver is harder to refine and also tends to corrode fairly quickly.

Much of Chimú art is highly decorative, such as large painted textiles designed to serve as a backdrop for activities occurring in front of them. Many of Chan Chan's long *ciudadela* walls bore no designs save for a single coat of red paint. Other friezes at the site consist of simple bands of horizontal lines or repeating motifs of fish, birds, or a squirrel-like animal that might be a nutria or coypu (see illustrations on pages 155 and 157). The depiction of spondylus divers is thus a rare exception, underscoring the importance of the shell for the lords of Chimú and the apparent obsession with the spiny oyster. Chimú artists continued the Lambayeque penchant for black ceramics with simple designs, but the symbolic content decreased, because the Sicán Lord was no longer popular. Large feather capes and shirts, garments adorned with glittering gold plaques, and other spectacular objects were the exclusive rights of the élite. The nobles often used or drank from gold and silver vessels that were replicas of ceramic vessels used by the common folk.

The Chimú empire stretched from near the modern Ecuador–Peru border southward. The fortress of Paramonga, standing high above the Fortaleza River, 120 miles (200km) north of modern Lima, has been suggested by some as marking the

LEFT

A Chimú tunic. The repeated pattern of stylized birds shares the decorative aesthetic of much art of the period. The figures in the inverted pyramid design, below the neck slit, may be monkeys or a variant of the "Moon Animal."

BELOW

Peru's dry coastal desert preserves not only textiles and wood, but also leather. To judge by the gold and turquoise ornaments and the delicate, lace-like, cutwork of the straps, these sandals belonged to someone of high status.

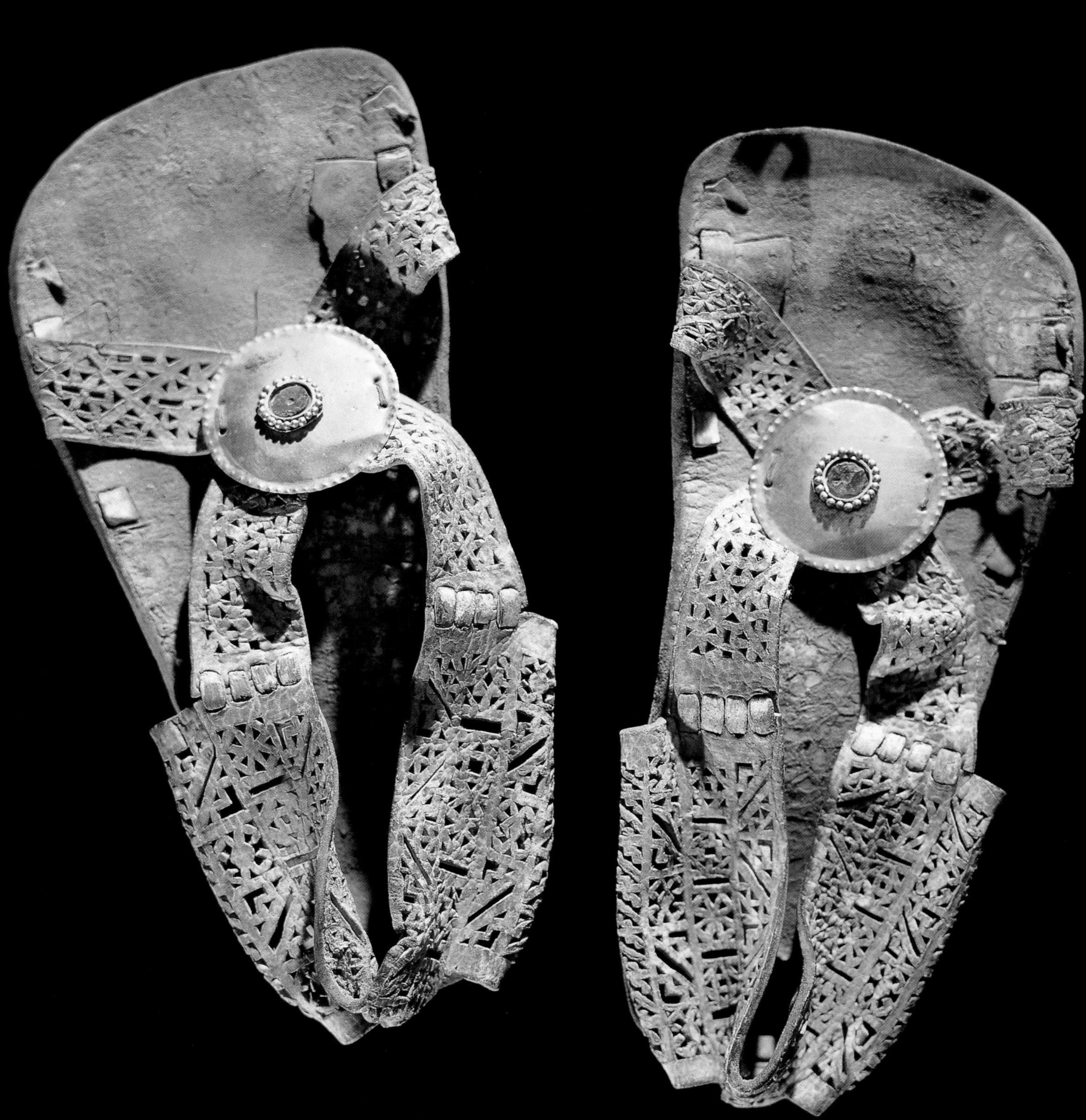

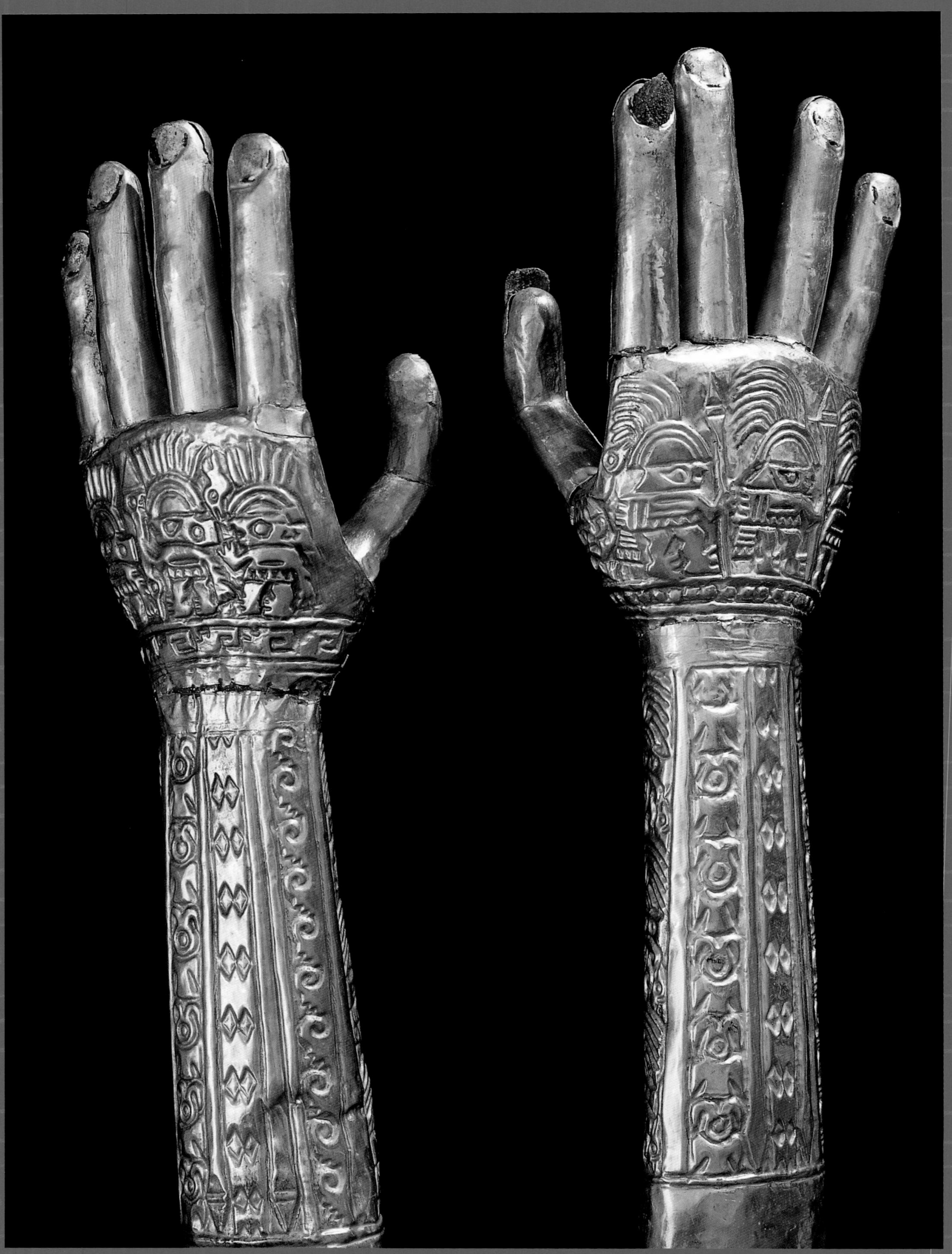

LEFT
Large gold hands and forearms, such as these Chimú examples, are of uncertain purpose. One suggestion is that they could have been worn as part of the ceremonial regalia of officiants at rituals, enabling them to appear larger than life.

RIGHT
A ceremonial Chimú feathercloth headdress. Found in Peru's central coastal region, its exotic bird feathers—including flamingo, macaw, Amazonian parrot, and razor-billed curassow—are evidence of trans-Andean trade networks.

frontier of the Chimú (see illustration, page 158), but it may have stretched further. Although no site rivaled Chan Chan, other administrative centers have been located, such as those at Manchan and Farfán.

CHIMÚ EXPANSION AND CONFRONTATION

Much smaller than the Chicama valley to its north, the Moche River valley must have been stretched to its limits to take care of the needs of the vast populace of the capital. Walk-in wells, as found in the *ciudadelas*, tapped a relatively low water table, but likely proved insufficient over time. The Chimú achieved some remarkable engineering feats, building a huge wall across the northern end of their valley, perhaps to control population movements into and out of their overstretched capital. To ease their water shortage they embarked on one of the largest canal construction projects in ancient South America. They reclaimed old canals in an attempt to build a massive channel, 44 miles (70km) long, from the mid-Chicama valley to Chan Chan. The project was never completed, as the builders could not make water run uphill across an active fault line in the desert.

The Chimú may have tried to build an empire on trade but they also employed military might. They appear to have become even more militaristic following another severe El Niño episode of floods and devastation that occurred in around 1100CE. It was at this point that the Chimú empire reached its greatest extent, conquering the valleys to its north. With its new strategy underway, the kingdom of Chimor rapidly expanded to become the second largest empire to exist in the preconquest Andes. However, it was soon to meet its match in an even greater power. Based far to the south, this new empire was ruled by a people who have come to be called the Inca.

LEFT

In a continent without draught animals until the arrival of Europeans, lords traveled on the shoulders of other humans. This panel from a Chimú palanquin features small structures filled with warriors, as if emphasizing the power of the ruler who once rode inside it. They may in fact be representations of the Sicán Lord, subsumed into Chimú iconography when the Lambayeque culture fell under the rule of Chimor.

chapter 6

THE INCA: MASTERS OF THE FOUR QUARTERS

THE LATE HORIZON

CA. 1450CE–CA. 1534CE

LEFT
The royal estate settlement of Machu Picchu has become a symbol of Inca civilization known today throughout the world. Believed to have been established by the Inca emperor Pachacuti in about 1450, the site's remoteness afforded it protection in the wake of the Spanish conquest and it remained untouched by outsiders until modern times.

THE EMPIRE OF THE SUN

THE ANDES UNDER INCA RULE

BELOW AND OPPOSITE
The elaborate figure painting on this Inca *kero* suggests it may date to the early Colonial Period, but even so the form continues earlier traditions. The detail (opposite) shows the Inca fascination with peoples of the tropical lowlands, here depicted with large feather headdresses, bows, and arrows.

The Inca have variously been called boring bureaucrats, the ideal socialists of the New World, Native American fascists, and South American Romans. They were none of these, of course, but it is easy to see how such interpretations—which arose to suit the political agendas of Westerners writing about them—came to be. In their detailed and methodical systems of accounting for their herds, fields, and subjects, the Inca can be seen as plodding administrators. With their highly orchestrated distribution of resources throughout the realm they may appear to have practiced an advanced form of socialism—complete with its darker, "Big Brother," aspects, such as the close monitoring of populations, social engineering, and the ruthless suppression of rebellions. And, in developing a refined military strategy centered on roads and rapid communication, on highly organized armies, and on the bringing of a distinctly Inca way of life along with conquest, the Inca do, indeed, appear in a general way to resemble the Romans.

We know much more about the Inca than any other prehistoric South American people because in 1534 they stepped, unwillingly, into the light of history when the Spanish arrived with papers, books, and pens as well as swords, cannons, and disease. Because so much is known about them, there is a danger of too easily projecting backward, of interpreting earlier Andean cultures and civilizations through an Inca lens. Similarly, we must beware of seeing earlier events as inevitably culminating in the creation of the Inca empire, the largest state to emerge in the preconquest Andes.

Spanish and *mestizo* authors also had their own agendas in writing what they did, and often twisted what they heard to suit their own devices. At the same time, those Inca who recounted their histories to the Spanish also wished to spin their tales to their own advantage. To give just one example, the Inca claimed that before the rise of their empire Peru had been in total chaos, and that they had been on a civilizing mission among savages.

LEFT
A detail of an anonymous oil painting of the Inca royal succession, painted in 18th-century Cuzco. The Spanish recognized the lineage, and may have misinterpreted it in their attempt to manipulate successive heirs in the Colonial Period.

TRAVELERS FROM THE CAVE

Like many great cultures the Inca had more than one origin myth. One described the creation of the Inca people and the other recounted how they became an empire. The Inca claimed that their ancestors were not originally from the Cuzco valley, the heartland of their empire, but had been born of Inti, the Sun, at the ancient city of Tiwanaku. From there, four brother–sister pairs are said to have traveled underground, emerging eventually from the cave of Pacaritambo ("Cavern of Origin"), near Cuzco, to continue their journey, led by Manco Capac, the progenitor of the Inca emperors, and Mama Ocllo, his sister and wife. When a golden staff sank into the earth they halted to establish the seat of the Inca people—the Coricancha, the great Inca temple of Cuzco.

The second tale occurs later, when the Inca were one of many small states in the turbulent era of the Late Intermediate Period. Around 1438, according to some estimates, the Inca were imperiled by an invasion of their enemies, the Chanka. Details of the story vary but a key element is the rise of a young prince who refuses

OPPOSITE
The distinctive curved wall of the Coricancha, the most sacred temple in Cuzco, is still visible today. In Inca times the sun temple's beautiful masonry was hidden from view beneath a covering of gold—the Inca fashioned their finest stonework for the eyes of their deities, not humans. The stonework was exposed when the gold was stripped and carried off in hundreds of cartloads by the Spanish, who subsequently built the church and convent of Santo Domingo on top of the temple as a sign of conquest and dominion.

LEFT
A bronze Inca axe-mace. Under the Inca, metallurgy reached levels at which metal tools became widespread, although they were probably limited to the higher ranks of the military and nobility.

OPPOSITE, ABOVE
The so-called "Stone of the Twelve Angles" is a most famous tour de force of Inca masonry, still in place in Hatun Raumiyoc street, Cuzco. The stones in this wall are fitted so precisely that no mortar was required. Today, this wall is part of the palace of the archbishop of Cuzco, but it was once the royal palace of Inca Roca.

OPPOSITE, BELOW
The trapezoidal niches and entranceways characteristic of Inca architecture are seen here at Pisac, one of several high-altitude Urubamba valley settlements—which also include Machu Picchu, Ollantaytambo, and Winay Wayna—that exhibit some of the finest architectural achievements of the Inca .

to submit or retreat, rallies his soldiers, and decisively defeats the Chanka. In the aftermath of the battle, the young lord hears tales that in the heat of the fight the very stones of the fields had risen up to fight the Chanka. In gratitude he orders that the stones be collected and placed in shrines for veneration. He takes the name Pachacuti, which means "the world turned upside down." To this day the word is used in Quechua, the old Inca language still widely spoken in the highlands of Peru, to refer to earthquakes as well as political upheavals. Pachacuti truly was an overturner of the old, for it is he who is credited with turning the Inca from a city-state into an empire.

The Inca king list totals eleven or so rulers, with Pachacuti followed by only two more monarchs before the arrival of the Spanish. Thus, the Inca claimed to have conquered their empire—from present-day Santiago, Chile, to northern Ecuador—in little more than a century. Recently, some scholars have suggested that Inca expansion occurred at a slower pace under the earlier kings. It is likely that Pachacuti was a real, living king and that, like so many other monarchs, he rewrote history as well as made it. To further complicate matters, the names of the kings prior to Pachacuti may represent offices rather than individuals, while another theory suggests that the eight rulers before him may have been four pairs of joint rulers. While this cannot be proved, it is not unlikely because there is a strong Andean penchant for dual rulership, and shared leadership is found throughout Native American culture. The Inca conquest of so huge a region in so short a time seems astounding, but it was not unprecedented in history, as can be seen in the lightning-fast spread of Muslim warriors out of Arabia, or the earlier accomplishments of Alexander the Great.

IMPERIAL STRATEGIES

The Inca empire owed its success to a combination of military might and skillful diplomacy. However, the military prowess of the Inca was not solely due to their

LEFT
The Inca royal estate of Machu Picchu viewed from the southwest, from part-way up the taller peak of Huayna Picchu. The complex included residences for royalty and retainers, temples, baths, service areas, and agricultural terraces. After the fall of Cuzco to the Spanish in 1534 Machu Picchu served, along with other royal settlements on the steep slopes of the Urubamba valley, as a retreat for Inca exiles. Never reached by the conquistadors, Machu Picchu was eventually abandoned, to be discovered by outsiders only in 1911, when a Yale University expedition led by Hiram Bingham arrived at the site.

RIGHT, ABOVE
The Intihuatana, "Hitching Post of the Sun," the central feature at the sun temple in Machu Picchu and other Inca sun temples. The notched post recalls the Lanzón and Tello Obelisk of Chavín de Huantar and may have been an astronomical sighting device as well as a ritual object.

RIGHT, BELOW
Notwithstanding Machu Picchu's breathtaking setting among the mountain clouds high above the Urubamba river, the settlement actually stands at a lower altitude than Cuzco. It thus offered the ruling Inca and his court a respite from the sometimes harsh conditions of the imperial capital.

weapons—primarily lances, clubs, and slings—which in fact differed little from those of Chavín times. It was the organization of armies and their logistical support that was key to Inca victories. The Inca may also have been the first South Americans to give their troops uniforms. The Spanish noted a distinct checkerboard tunic design for warriors, and an Inca army on the advance must have been an impressive sight. More importantly, the Inca system of roads and storage facilities meant that armies could move quickly and still remain supplied with weapons and food.

The Inca probably integrated older road systems into their own network where they found them. On the coast, roads were wide and usually walled. In the highlands, paths were narrow but almost always paved with stones, thus ensuring easy travel. By the sixteenth century, the road system consisted of major highways running north–south along the coast and through the highlands, connected laterally by arterial branches in important coastal valleys. Large administrative towns, such as Huanuco Pampa, were centers of Inca control, housing civil servants, military units, and

LEFT
A long-haired llama worked in silver sheet metal underscores the nature of the Inca highland economy. Llamas cannot be ridden and were used instead as pack animals, often in large herds, in which role they became vital for transporting goods throughout the Inca empire.

ABOVE
The architectural complex of Ollantaytambo in the Urubamba valley was a combined residence, temple, and fortress. It is located on a mountain shoulder above the river and commands important passes. It is believed that Pachacuti had the site built using forced labour from the Lake Titicaca area. In later times Ollantaytambo was one of the places where the Inca court in exile held out against Spanish attacks from Cuzco. According to Spanish accounts, its terraces were planted with bright flowers.

artisans. Nearby storehouses contained both goods paid as taxes by local residents and food to be rationed to them in time of need. Smaller way-stations, known as *tambos*, dotted the Inca road system at intervals and near critical junctures, such as the famous rope bridges that spanned highland chasms.

Roads could be used by imperial armies but also by enemies. The Inca therefore maintained strict control over who could travel along their highways and failure to wear the costume of one's ethnic group, and thus be easily identified, was punishable by death. The Inca also instituted a special corps of highly trained messenger runners known as *chasquis*. In the absence of money, the Inca exacted taxes in the form of goods and services and in this way inducted the best runners among their subjects into the *chasqui* system. Wearing uniforms, they would run relatively short distances to pass oral messages or small objects to the next runner, often located at a *tambo*. In this way the Sapa Inca, the emperor or king, could receive news of events at the far end of his empire in only a few days—and also, it is claimed, fresh fish from the coast and snow from the mountaintops for his delectation.

RIGHT
Detail of a silver figurine of an unidentified male. Gold inlay encircles his headdress. Another inlay across his upper cheeks and nose has been lost, but the shell inlay on his upper chest and arms is also intact. The ear lobes, enlarged from wearing ear spools, indicate that the figure represents someone of high social status.

ABOVE
Detail of a tunic, probably *qompi,* the finest Inca cloth (see page 201). The distinctive square motif, or *tocapu,* may indicate the status of the person who wore the garment. This motif is one of those that appears on the royal garment shown on page 200, perhaps indicating the ruler's superiority over all other persons of high status.

The *chasquis* also carried *khipu*, knotted string records. Again, earlier examples of *khipu* are known but the Inca organized *khipu* recording on a large scale under another government bureau, the *khipukamayos*, which was responsible for making and maintaining *khipu* archives. Scholars are still endeavoring to understand the functioning of the *khipu* (which simply means "knot.") Drawings from the early Colonial Period show a cord held horizontally, with other cords hanging from it. It is known that the Inca used a decimal numerical system and that there was a hierarchy of cords, so that subcategories of recorded items would be noted on strings attached to others that carried higher categories of information. Grouping strings together, tying knots in different directions, and employing different colors of string were among the many ways in which information was stored using this method. *Khipu* were certainly used to keep accounting records, for example the ages, sexes, and wool colors of a herd of llamas, or the types of unit and their numbers in an army. However, there is growing evidence that *khipu* also recorded narratives, such as histories, although investigations into this are at an early stage.

BELOW

This *khipu* may have held particularly important information, judging by its wooden rack, which is relatively rare. The Inca numerical system was decimal. The clusters of knots at different levels of the cords are equivalent to place values in our written system.

LIFE UNDER INCA RULE

The Inca claimed that they brought civilization and true religion to those whom they conquered. Like the Romans, they offered peace and prosperity to those who willingly accepted their overlordship. Local *kurakas* (lords) were allowed to remain in power and their people could carry on worshipping their own gods, which would be granted the honor of being installed in a temple in Cuzco, the Inca capital. These local leaders were also integrated into the Inca system by being presented with fine textiles (the most valued material good) and sending their children to be educated at Cuzco into Inca ways. In return all they had to do was build an Inca sun temple, set aside land and resources for its maintenance, pay taxes to the Inca state, and, of course, remain loyal to the emperor. These favorable terms and rewards helped maintain control over any wayward *kuraka* who might decide to break free of the Inca yoke.

When local peoples resisted incorporation into the empire or, worse, rose in rebellion afterward, Inca retribution could be fierce. Inca armies rarely met defeat and once the contentious territory was firmly in imperial hands the state exercised close control. Even in tranquil areas the Inca imposed a hierarchical system in which the population was divided into units, beginning with a single unit of ten households and working upward into larger units. All were under the gaze of imperial officials who employed spies and reported infractions to their superiors. Taxes were taken in the form not only of crops and livestock but also artisans' skills and other services. Good runners would become *chasquis* (see above), and the prettiest girls would be pressed into Inca service as *acllacuna*, "chosen women," to weave, make *chicha* beer for festivals, and, occasionally, be presented as gifts from the emperor. When the

BELOW
The Inca prized maize, especially for making *chicha*. Gold and silver life-size replicas of important plants and animals filled a garden in the Coricancha. This might even be a fragment of that fabulous creation.

RIGHT
The Inca occasionally sacrificed children, perhaps to appease mountain deities. In 1999 these clothed Inca silver figurines were found near the almost perfectly preserved bodies of three child sacrifices, close to the summit of Mount Llullaillaco in Argentina.

Inca conquered the Chimú they are said to have deported the last king, Minchançamon, from Chan Chan to Cuzco together with his royal artisans and the best women weavers of his kingdom.

The most recalcitrant rebel areas might suffer a deportation of the entire population to another part of the empire. Known as *mitimae*s, these groups would be placed in an alien environment, surrounded by local residents who would not welcome their presence. To give but one example, the present-day Salasaca of the southern Ecuadorian highlands claim to have been *mitimae*s moved by the Inca from Lake Titicaca. Their weaving designs still use *altiplano* motifs.

CAUSES FOR CONQUEST

The reasons for Inca imperial expansion have been the subject of debate for some time. The expansion appears to have been another example of the continuing oscillation in the Andes between periods of relatively large but independent kingdoms and chiefdoms followed by the rise of highland conquest societies. The anthropologist Robert Carneiro has pointed out that population growth and demographic pressure would have occurred more quickly in the highlands than on the coast. Narrow valleys would more quickly reach their maximum capacity for any expansion of irrigation or intensification of labor in the fields. The critical point at which a community had either to conquer or to perish would therefore occur sooner than in coastal valleys, where there was more potential room for growth. Rulers of expanding highland populations would have been encouraged to "leap-frog" over the tall mountains to conquer neighboring valleys facing the same pressures.

Another explanation for Inca imperialism was developed by Arthur Demarest and Geoffrey Conrad. The Inca told the Spanish that upon his death, each Sapa Inca was mummified and treated as if he were still living. He would be offered food, his

ABOVE
This sculpted stone at Sayhuite depicts a miniature landscape with buildings, patios, and other features. It was likely used for Inca rituals that perhaps included liquid offerings running along its carved canals.

rich clothes were changed daily, and he was spoken to and consulted as if he were still alive. His entire household, known as a *panaca*, which consisted of a huge number of people related to him, would continue to live in his palace and estates. The next king, whether a son or not, would preside over a different *panaca* and have to find new lands and wealth to support his prestige indefinitely, both during his lifetime and after his death. Thus, each succeeding emperor would have been encouraged to conquer or incorporate new territories into the empire. Given that the Inca nobility had inter-

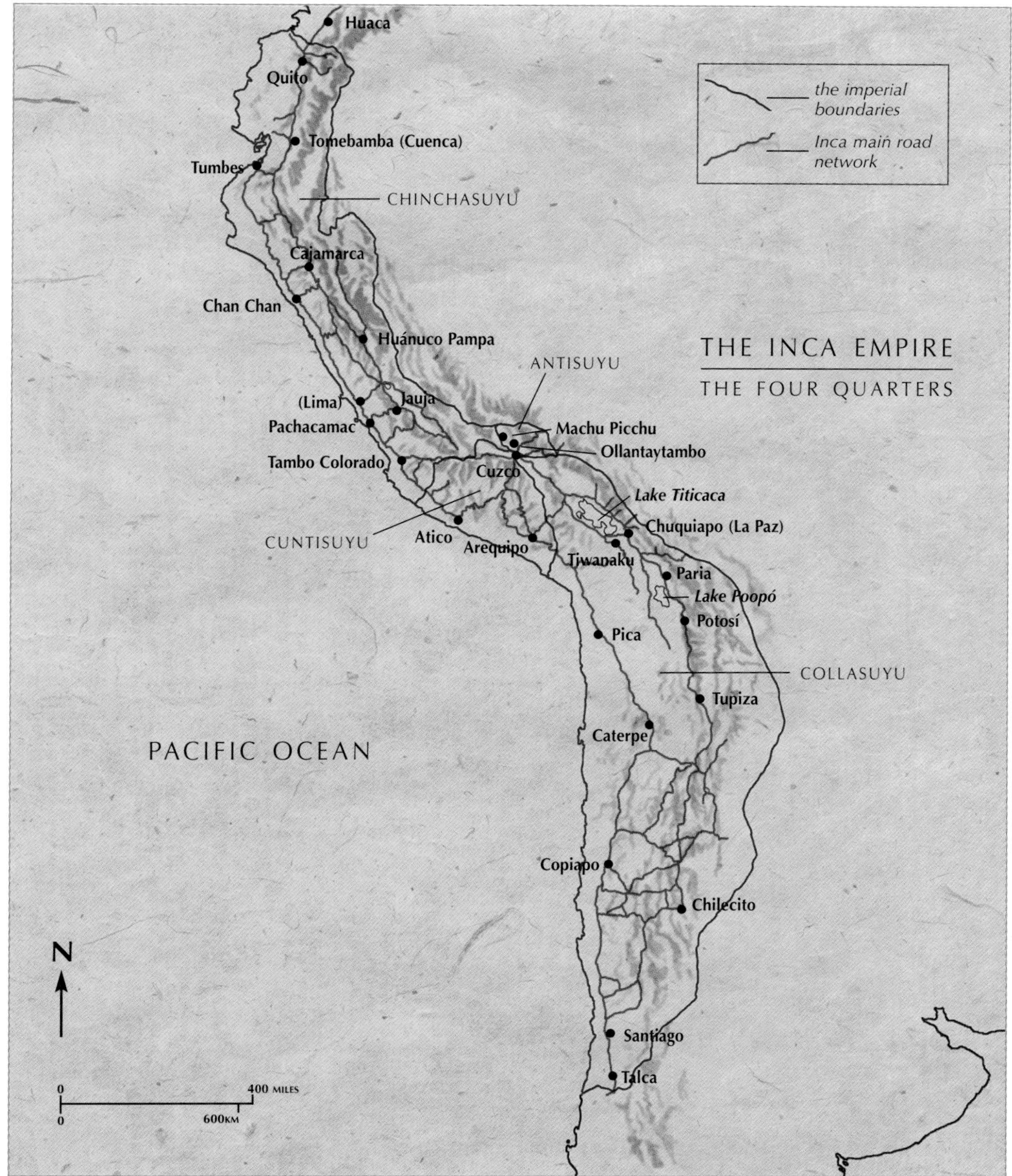

LEFT

The map shows the Inca empire at its greatest extent, under Huayna Capac, who ruled mostly from the second city of Tomebamba (modern Cuenca). The Inca realm was divided into four *suyus* that emanated from the capital at Cuzco: Chinchasuyu (running northwest from Cuzco up into modern Ecuador), Antisuyu (northeast), Cuntisuyu (southwest), and Collasuyu (running southeast into modern Chile). Measured along the coast, Inca influence extended for some 3,000 miles (5,000km). Within the empire there was a vast, well-engineered road system that facilitated central administration and an efficient economy. The two main highways ran north–south in parallel, one down the coast and the other inland. Many lateral routes connected them. The entire network contained more than 14,000 miles (22,500km) of roads, often running across difficult terrain.

married over time, we might expect many shared relatives, so how new *panaca*s were formed, and how close ties might have affected this system, is a topic remaining to be explored. For example, if a woman was the wife of one Sapa Inca and the mother of his successor, to which *panaca* would she belong? Whether this system was original to the Inca or was borrowed from the Chimú is uncertain, but it does fit with known facts about the fascinating Inca religious system, which was intimately bound up with Inca statecraft and the very form of the empire itself.

SHAPERS OF THE COSMOS

OPPOSITE, ABOVE
The magnificent terraces of Winay Wayna were made with an eye to their aesthetic as well as agricultural function. The site was one of many imperial estates in the Inca heartland of the Urubamba Valley, home to Cuzco and Machu Picchu.

OPPOSITE, BELOW
Concentric terraces at Moray, a ceremonial site near Cuzco, follow the typical Inca pattern of imposing order on the Andean landscape while at the same time respecting its natural contours.

The Inca were experts at imposing order not only on their capital city (see pages 190–193) but also on the "natural" world around them. The Andes take their name from the Spanish word *andenes* (platforms, terraces) because, in valley after valley, the conquerors came across astonishing terraces of fields rising up from the river to the heights. The terraces significantly increased the amount of land that could be placed under cultivation, and the Inca carefully composed the soil within them to improve drainage and maximize the efficiency of irrigation canals. The Inca took terracing to a great art and today, in many valleys, the land under cultivation ends well below the ancient Inca terraces, which rise above the modern fields. Terraces usually followed the natural contours of the hills and slopes, making a completely artificial landscape somehow appear entirely natural. There can be little doubt that in many cases the terraces were designed for their aesthetic impact as well as their practical function, as for example at sites in the Urubamba valley such as Winay Wayna (see illustration, right), Moray, and Ollantaytambo (see page 180). In the case of the last, Spanish accounts claimed that the terraces were filled not with crops but with flowers. If these reports are true, the visual effect of such a pleasure garden must have been stunning.

The Inca conceived of their land as having four divisions or provinces (*suyu*) of unequal size that were centered on the capital of Cuzco, which has led some to attribute to the entity the name Tawantinsuyu, or "The Land of the Four Quarters." The four quarters were understood as indispensable parts of a greater whole. Drawing on ancient Andean beliefs and practices, the Inca saw reality in terms of a dynamic asymmetric dualism, in which the slightly different sized members of a pair were intimately bound to and dependent on each other. This ideology was expressed in many ways, from the relations between men and women to the almost (but not quite) equally sized *kero*s which were employed in state rituals to establish political alliances. However, the number of pairs involved in such relationships could be many.

CUZCO: NAVEL OF THE COSMOS

The most elaborate manifestation of Inca dualistic ideology is found in their capital city of Cuzco, thought of as a navel, the center around which, both literally and figuratively, the empire and the world itself were ordered. At Cuzco's center was a plaza composed of two sections: the larger Huacapayta plaza of Hanan (Upper) Cuzco and the smaller Cusipayta plaza of Hurin (Lower) Cuzco. The principal division of the city into Hanan Cuzco and Hurin Cuzco followed the topography of the sloping valley floor. In the plaza—which was much larger in preconquest times than today—stood an altar-throne, probably representing a mountain, for the monarch to perform the holiest imperial rites. Close by was a hole connected to an underground canal, for the pouring of copious amounts of *chicha* offerings. The plaza floor was

BELOW
The entrance to the fortress complex of Sacsahuaman, the "Puma's Head" of Cuzco (see plan, opposite). This citadel guarded the Inca capital on flat tableland, its only vulnerable flank. Work was initiated by Pachacuti, who had rebuilt Cuzco. The carefully fitted irregular stone blocks of which the wall is constructed are typical of the Inca polygonal masonry used when producing massive dimensions.

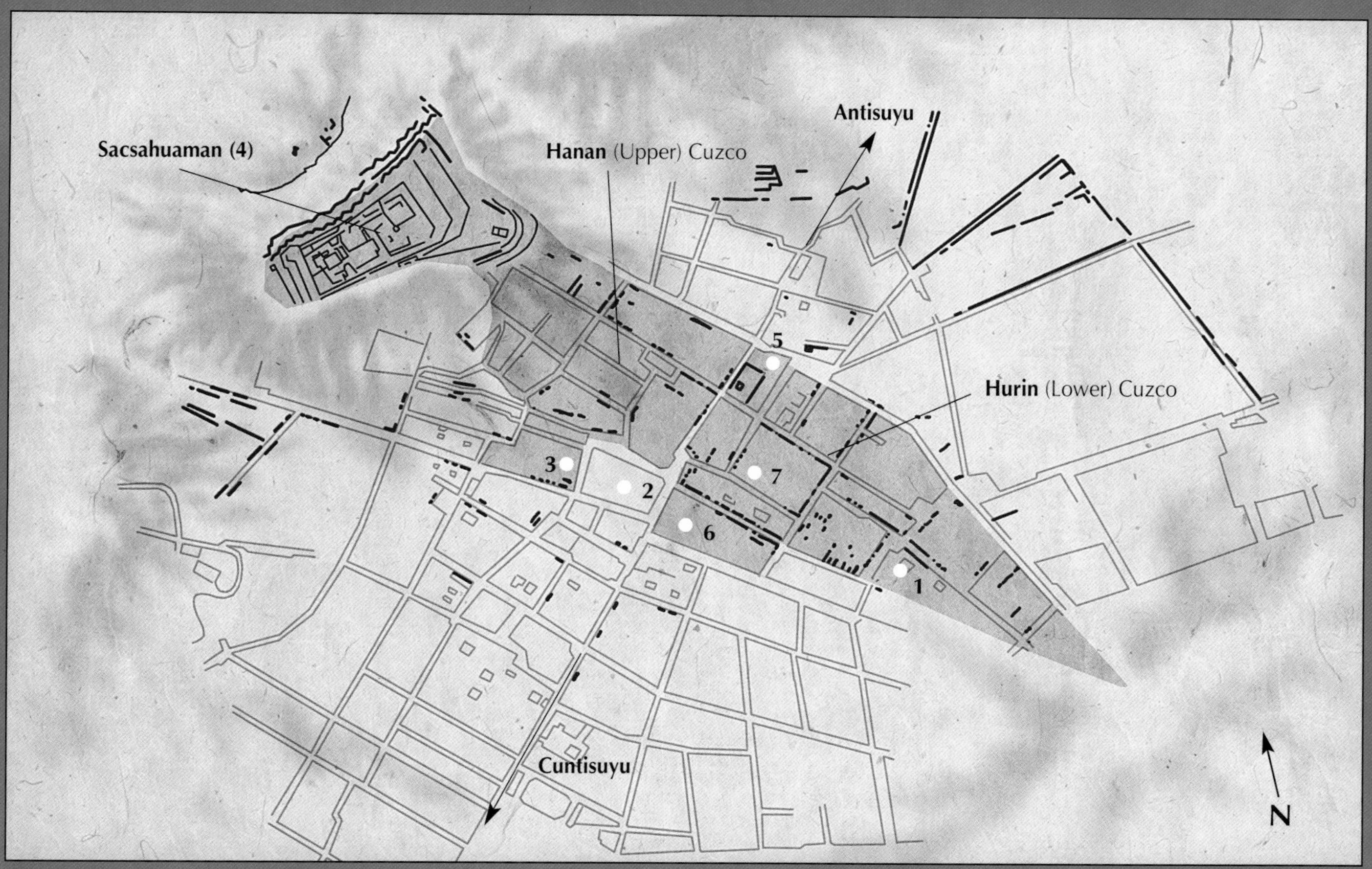

ABOVE
A plan of Cuzco. Some 41 *ceques* (invisible lines of sacred power), radiated from the Coricancha (1). Facing the Huacapayta, or great plaza (2), was Pachacuti's palace (3). In the mid-1400s he drained a swamp to create Hanan (Upper) Cuzco and initiated works at Sacsahuaman (4). In Hurin (Lower) Cuzco stood the palaces of Inca Roca, Huayna Capac, and Tupa Inca Yupanqui respectively (5, 6, 7). Planned around two now covered rivers, the city's central districts have been claimed to form the shape of a puma (delineated above), of which Sacsahuaman is the head.

covered with sand from distant beaches, so that the chief geographical components of the empire—from coast to mountains—were also symbolically present.

From the plaza radiated the four principal roads and axes of the empire, dividing the realm into four parts: Antisuyu (northeast), Collasuyu (southeast), Cuntisuyu (southwest), and Chinchasuyu (northwest), each named for the major cultural group of its region. These roads did not follow the cardinal directions but the intercardinal ones. At the height of the empire, the system resulted in two large provinces, Collasuyu and Chinchasuyu, and two smaller ones, perhaps reflecting the same idea of unequal pairs seen in the city itself. The orientation also encompassed the shifting position of the Milky Way in the South American night sky. The ethnographer Gary Urton has documented modern Quechua understandings of this "celestial river," the orientation of which shifts from northeast–southwest to northwest–southeast during the year. The Inca, the ancestors of today's Quechua speakers, were almost certainly aware of this shifting and so linked heavenly patterns with their earthly realm. But they also elaborated the ties between nature and culture in an even more sophisticated system.

PRECEDING PAGES
Sacsahuaman's massive three-tiered defensive walls were constructed from enormous blocks of quarried stone transplanted and fitted together. The walls were built in a zigzag design to provide opportunities for crossfire. The Inca and Spanish met here in the decisive battle for Cuzco in 1534.

ABOVE
This distinctively Inca tin bronze head represents a puma or similar feline and was probably once the finial on a staff of office. The puma was a prestigious Inca royal and aristocratic emblem—and, of course, the animal that was identified with the city of Cuzco.

THE TEMPLE OF GOLD

Another nodal point in Cuzco was the Coricancha, the "Golden Compound" that was the holiest temple in the realm, a shrine for the worship of the sun, and home of a fabled garden in which a man, a woman, animals, and plants were exquisitely rendered in gold and silver. From the temple there radiated 41 imaginary lines, called *ceques*, which ran through 328 *huacas* (sacred sites such as caves, rocks, and springs), pillars, and other important points on the landscape, such as critical junctions of irrigation canals. Spanish chroniclers made detailed records of the points on the *ceque* lines, which theoretically extended to infinity. However, the archaeologist Brian Bauer has demonstrated that *ceques* do not actually extend in straight lines if all the *huacas* are followed. It is likely that over time new points were added to the system, so that the lines sometimes veered from their intended direction.

Ceque lines may have been organized into the four-quarter system and also grouped in patterns associated with a lunar calendar. Debate and research continues into the detailed organization and operation of the *ceques*, but it is clear that the rituals at the hundreds of sites on the lines were carried out throughout the year, sequentially, each *ceque* in turn, like the sweep of the shadow on a sundial, so that a calendrical component was part of the system. It is clear, too, that the incorporation of *huacas* into a *ceque* integrated the people for whom these local sites were important into the larger Inca plan, compressing history, religion, earth, sky, time, and space into a single cosmological system.

Cuzco was a holy place and not an ordinary city. Emperors, priests, perhaps artisans, and various retinues and embassies lived there. Over the years, different emperors built their own palaces and temples. Although severely damaged by wars and time, many original buildings still remain and the street plan of the center is not

ABOVE
The so-called "Seat of the Inca" at Sacsahuaman exemplifies Inca ideals and ideology in stone, as sharp-edged platforms emerge from natural rock. The exact use of the feature is unknown.

greatly changed from Inca times. As New York City is "The Big Apple," Cuzco was, among many names, "The Big Puma." The puma's "head" was the temple-fortress of Sacsahuaman, high above the city on tableland that was crucial to the city's defense. At the other, lower, end of the city is a district still known today as Pumachupan, "The Puma's Tail," where two channeled rivers came together. This was another point of power, because it was a *tinkuy*—a place where two things join and become one. The streets of the central area of the city were reported by early Spanish chroniclers to have been laid out in the form of the puma's body (see diagram, page 191), although to a modern viewer this form appears to be rather forced.

The city was adorned with the finest Inca masonry. Stonemasons were masters of their craft, able to carve stone in a huge variety of ways, from apparently "crude" rough blocks that in reality fitted together with great precision, to perfect rectilinear blocks that fitted so closely—and without mortar—that a knife blade cannot be inserted between them. Many examples remain visible to this day (see illustrations on pages 172, 175, 190, and 192–193).

FASHIONING NATURE

INCA ART AND AESTHETICS

OPPOSITE
Inca weavers were as skilled as any in the Andes, as this finely made bag demonstrates. The highland climate affords poor preservation, and most surviving examples of Inca textiles have been found either on the coast or frozen at very high altitudes.

An intentional blurring of the distinction between what we would consider "natural" and "cultural" forms is one of the key components of Inca aesthetics and statecraft. At a number of sites, precise geometric carving appears to blend with, or emerge from, rough natural formations. For example, at Qenqo, an important shrine on a *ceque* line near Cuzco, a rock terrace was built around a large natural monolith that resembled a puma. The surface of a larger boulder behind it was intricately carved with stylized animals, plants, and cityscapes without altering the general form of the rock. Similar sculpted boulders have been found elsewhere (see illustration, page 186). While practical in function, the zigzag form of the defensive walls of Sacsahuaman, the citadel of Cuzco, also appears to echo the hills behind.

RIGHT
Three gold figurines of two females and a male. Such objects served funerary purposes and were made in gold, silver, and spondylus shell, three precious substances of the Inca.

RIGHT

This gold figurine deviates from the standard Inca form and may have served different purposes. For the Inca, the essence of the material was more important than its display. Covering it with paint was quite acceptable; in fact it only enriched the object.

BELOW
A vase of terracotta shaped like a fish, from the late Inca period. It can be thus identified by certain iconographic attributes, such as the neck of the vase and the decoration representing fish scales. The Inca road network meant that the inhabitants of Cuzco received fresh fish to eat.

This interest in playing with natural forms was the expression of an empire which, while fully an artifice of the political ambitions of the lords of Cuzco, wished to present itself as an inevitable, completely natural state of being. The skill of the Inca in this regard was employed in their holiest sanctuary, the Coricancha in Cuzco, not only in the golden garden (see pages 184 and 194) but also in a series of gold statues in human shape representing the various stages of the sun—which some have conceptualized as the respective human life stages of child, adult, and old man—passing from early morning to high noon and sunset. Realistic depictions of living creatures and plants are known in precious metal and other media (see, for example, illustrations on pages 178, 184, and 202), but otherwise the Inca chose what we might consider fairly abstract styles for much of their art.

Following trends of the Late Intermediate Period, the Inca mass-produced ceramics such as *urpu*, standardized *chicha* storage vessels, on a huge scale. The best are beautifully made and commonly decorated with simple, well-executed motifs. Metalworking extended beyond gold and silver to include extensive production in

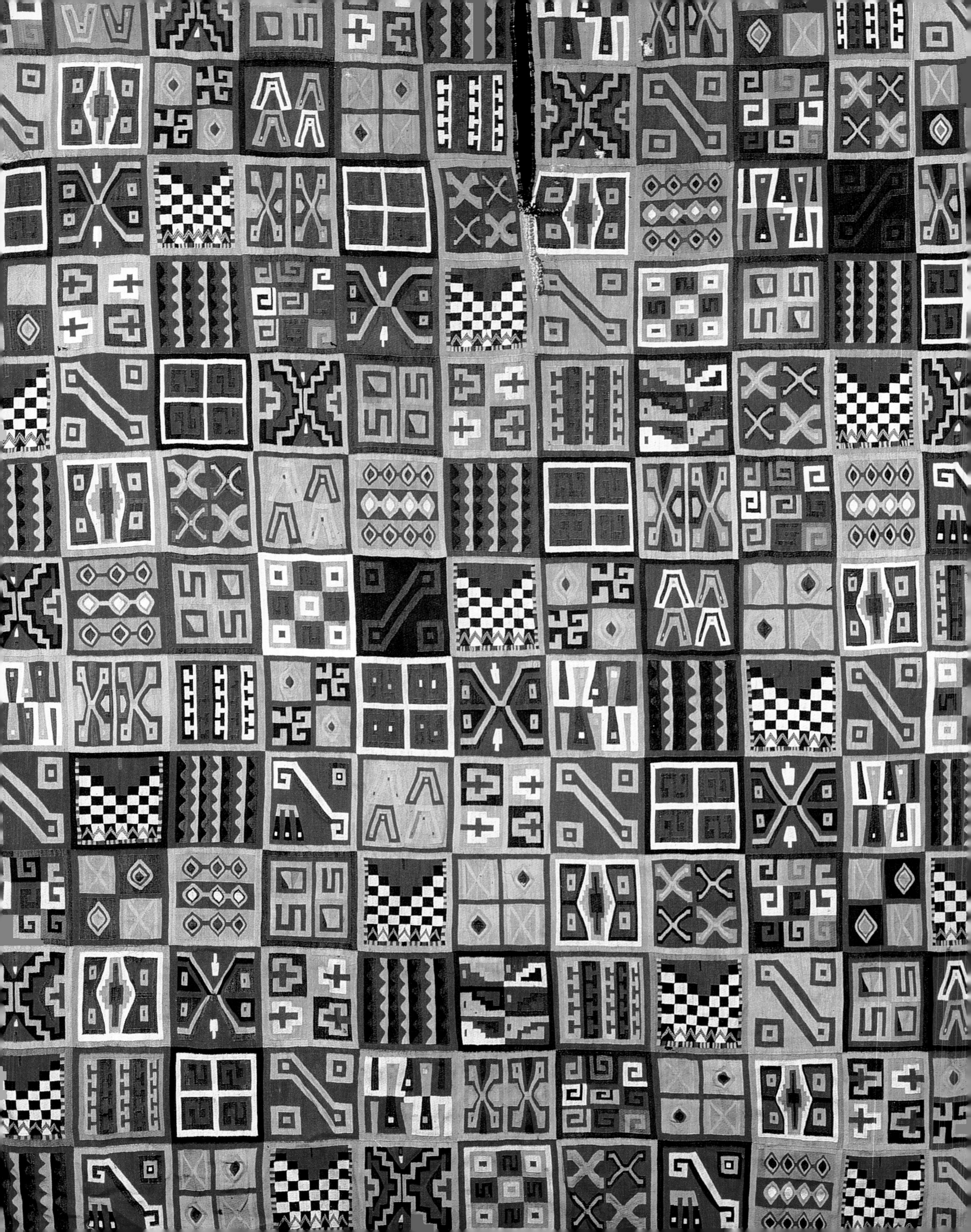

bronze of objects including utilitarian items such as tweezers, beads, and tools. By late Inca times these appear to have been increasingly widespread, beyond a narrow group of the élite, although how common they were is still unclear.

Spondylus still retained its sacred value, lapis lazuli was brought from faraway Chile, and precious tropical bird feathers were obtained from the warm lands below the Inca highlands. But the most precious goods were textiles. The best fabric was called *qompi*, woven from finely spun camelid fiber by the *acllacuna*, the imperial "chosen women," for royal and ritual use. *Qompi* attained incredible counts of several hundred threads per centimeter. Other textiles were also highly valued, such as feather cloaks and tunics adorned with metal plaques, and Atahualpa, the last Inca emperor, is known to have possessed a garment woven from bat hair.

Government officials wore garments that were distinctive in both color and design. We know through a variety of sources that square geometric designs (*tocapu*) adorned tunics of various ranks of civil service officers and that they served some kind of identifying function. It has been pointed out that *tocapu* designs bear little

ABOVE
A simple but valuable spondylus shell necklace found on the body of an Inca boy sacrificed on Mount Llullailaco (see also page 185).

OPPOSITE
An all-*tocapu* tunic. Miniature checkerboard military tunics with red bibs are scattered throughout the design, as is a motif similar to that on page 182. The complete covering of the tunic with *tocapu* suggests that this may well have been a royal garment, as lesser officials wore tunics with only a few bands of the designs.

ABOVE
Fancy drinking vessels called *paccha* were popular late in Inca times and into the Colonial Period. This one, in the form of an armadillo, reflects the Inca fascination with the people and creatures of the dense and mysterious tropical regions, which were thought to be repositories of great spiritual power.

resemblance to motifs of earlier cultures, as if to make plain the unprecedented domination of the Inca over the Andean world. In the early Colonial Period, Guamán Poma de Ayala depicted Inca rulers wearing tunics that were covered entirely with *tocapu* (see page 200). *Tocapu* are found in other media as well, including on buildings and *keros*, and may have been a kind of signing system that perhaps even approached a quasi-hieroglyphic form. In any event, *tocapu* were clearly an aid to the management of the Inca civil service and bureaucracy, together with the armies, roads, *khipu*, and taxation systems.

The Inca created and maintained an empire with great skill for a hundred years before they met a challenge that was impossible for them to have foreseen—a challenge literally from beyond their world. The arrival of European conquerors in person was preceded by a disastrous epidemic of smallpox, one of the diseases that they had

brought with them to the Americas and to which Andean peoples, like other Native Americans, had almost no immunity. The result was a calamity for the Inca, whose empire rapidly collapsed. Perhaps the empire was already stretched to its limit, given the tools and methods available for managing it, and would soon have fallen apart even without the twin disasters of disease and conquest. It is something to which we will never know the answer. What is certain is that within another century the peoples and cultures of Peru were profoundly and irrevocably changed.

BELOW
An elaborate late Inca or early Colonial Period *paccha*. The liquid was poured into the bowl at the end, flowing through the animals and along the sinuous channel to the drinker's mouth. The stem is painted with the *cantata*, the Inca royal flower.

LEFT

Tambo Colorado was an Inca administrative center in the lower Pisco River valley, on the south coast. A way-station (*tambo*) controlling communications between the coast and the highlands, it was built entirely of adobe and bears all the hallmark features of Inca architecture. These include trapezoidal openings and niches, and compounds consisting of rooms set around an inner courtyard, the compounds in turn surrounding a trapezoidal central plaza. The site took its name ("Red Way-station") from its red-painted adobe walls.

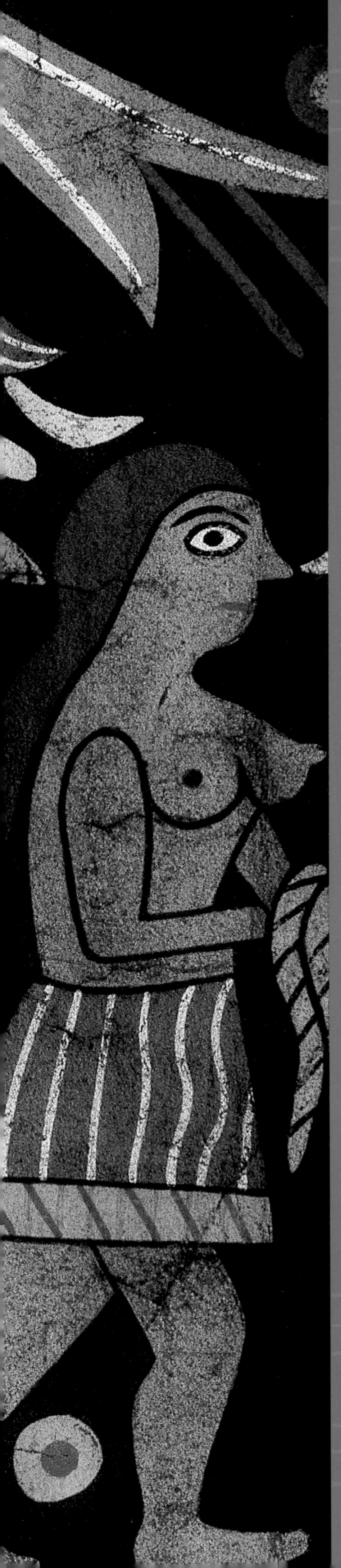

chapter 7

A WORLD TURNED UPSIDE DOWN

EPILOGUE: THE CONQUEST AND AFTER

LEFT
This detail from a painted wooden *kero* of the Colonial Period depicts an Inca with a captive woman. Colonial Period native art often celebrated the past glories of the Inca empire, while finding ways to please or accommodate new social and political realities.

THE EAGLE AND THE CONDOR

THE COLLAPSE OF THE INCA WORLD

Sitting in his litter, gazing across the emerald green agricultural terraces in northern Chinchasuyu, Sapa Inca Huayna Capac knew that there was much with which he could be pleased. His great-grandfather, Pachacuti, had founded the Inca empire and subsequent rulers had extended its dominion, while Huayna Capac himself had conquered these far northern territories, his favorite lands. Here, in what we now know as Ecuador, he had built a palace, Tumibamba, and fathered many brave sons from the maidens he had taken as wives. Far below the emperor, the workers on the terraced fields appeared tiny, like the fleas which the poorest of his subjects picked from their heads to give the imperial tax collectors—for all must give something, however small, to the Inca who had brought peace and prosperity to the land. And the

RIGHT
Manco Capac Inca, the mythical founder of the Inca dynasty, was portrayed as the son of the Sun in this 18th-century painting of the Cuzco School. The style has been recognized as a significant achievement of early colonial art.

four provinces of the Inca domain had expanded this far in only a hundred years. How much farther might the empire extend in the years to come?

But around that time, as recorded later by Spanish chroniclers, a number of strange phenomena were reported in the Inca empire. An eagle attacked a condor. A red light the color of blood encircled the moon. A comet—traditionally an evil omen—burned brightly. And Huayna Capac dreamt that three dwarves entered his room. These signs were taken as portents of doom. The year was 1529.

In Panama, less distant from Huayna Capac than the southernmost end of his empire, a plot to seize the wealth of Peru was already under way. Francisco Pizarro had come to the New World from Spain as a young man. Illiterate, he and his four half-brothers were as arrogant as they were poor but they were also fiercely ambitious. Pizarro had become wealthy in the Isthmus through trade in cattle and slaves. He had also learned how to conquer an empire through the tales he had heard of Hernan Cortés in Mexico: find translators, employ Indian allies, and capture the king. In November 1524, Pizarro and his partner, Diego de Almagro, formed an expedition

ABOVE
The towers of Cuzco Cathedral, left, and the Jesuit Church of the Society of Jesus, bathed in the afternoon light, dominate a corner of the central plaza of Cuzco, the former Inca capital. The first stone for the cathedral was laid in 1559 but the construction was not completed until 1669. It stands on the site of an Inca palace and much of the building stone was acquired from Sacsahuaman. Both churches exemplify the Colonial Spanish Baroque style.

ABOVE
A roll-out rendering of a *kero* decoration that depicts Inca troops, armed with stone-tipped battle-axes, fighting Spaniards. A neo-Inca state, based in the tropical forest near Cuzco, continued to resist the Spanish as late as the 1570s.

that set sail on a two-year voyage, reaching the region of the modern Peru–Ecuador border in 1526 and capturing two Indians to train as translators. Six more years passed in preparation for the conquest that began in late 1532.

A WORLD TURNED UPSIDE DOWN

In the months following Huayna Capac's musings at Tumibamba, his lands were struck by a great plague so devastating that death rates were as high as eighty percent or more in some areas. The disease is usually thought to have been smallpox, traveling faster through the Americas than the Europeans who had brought it to the New World nearly

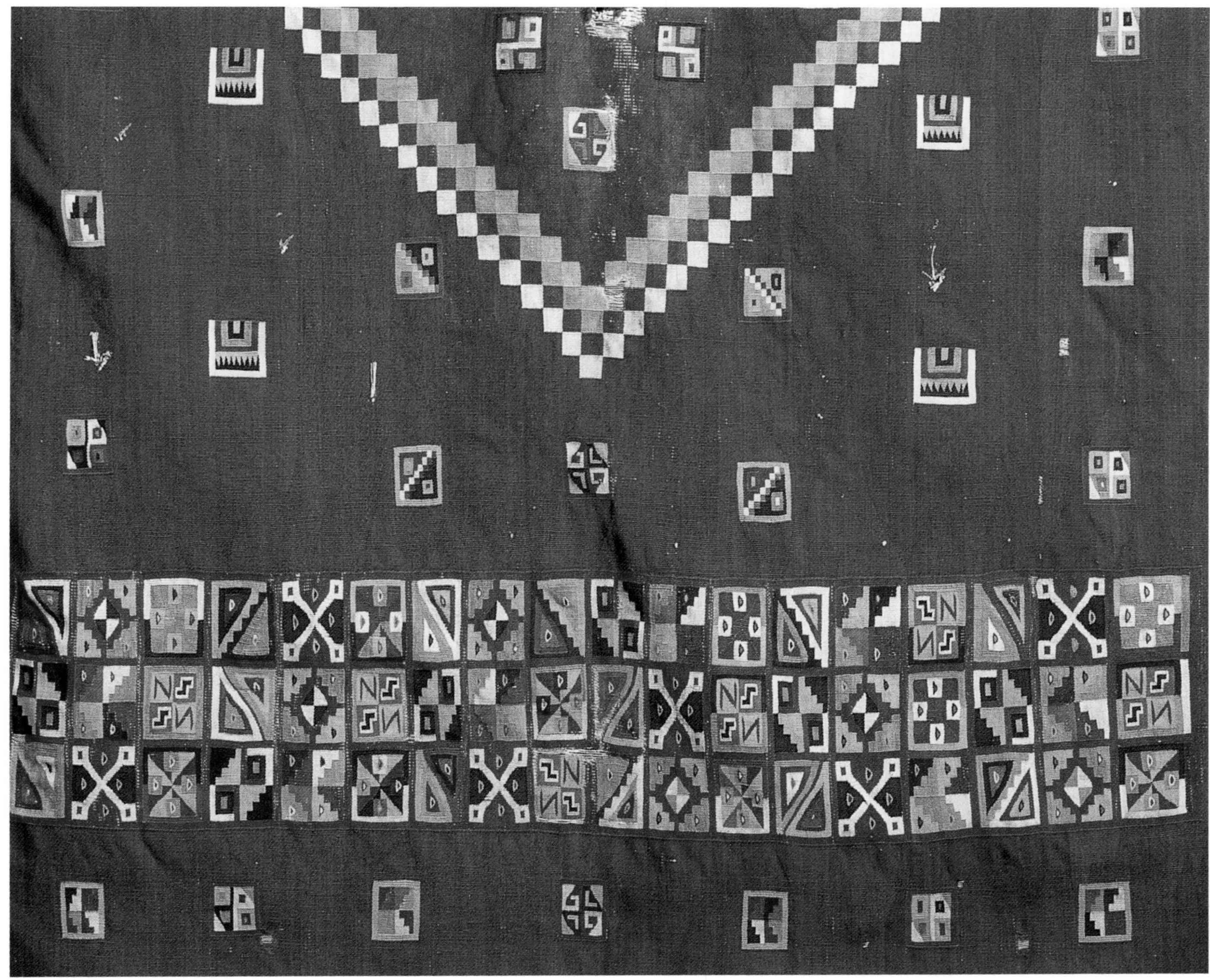

ABOVE
Finely woven Inca-style *uncus* (tunics) continued to be made and worn well into the Colonial Period, often at Christian festivals, such as Corpus Christi. The combination of red and blue fabrics and the stepped yoke were symbols of Inca royalty continued from imperial times.

four decades earlier. The pandemic had a seriously destabilizing effect on Inca society. As well as wiping out much of the population, the plague also affected the royal succession when, probably in 1530, Huayna Capac succumbed, as did his designated heir. The Inca empire was thrown into a civil war between Huascar, of a southern (Cuzco) faction, and Atahualpa from Ecuador. Atahualpa had gained the upper hand when Pizarro and his band arrived in 1532 and inserted themselves into the fray.

Atahualpa headed for Cajamarca, a city still famous today for its healing bath waters, but the Spaniards had got there first and were lying in wait for the new Sapa Inca. They captured Atahualpa in the main plaza of the city and proceeded to demand

RIGHT
A 1594 colored engraving of Cuzco, the Inca capital city, by Georgius Braun. Made by someone who had never been to South America, the image and plan are typical of the idealized, romanticized views of the New World held by some Europeans.

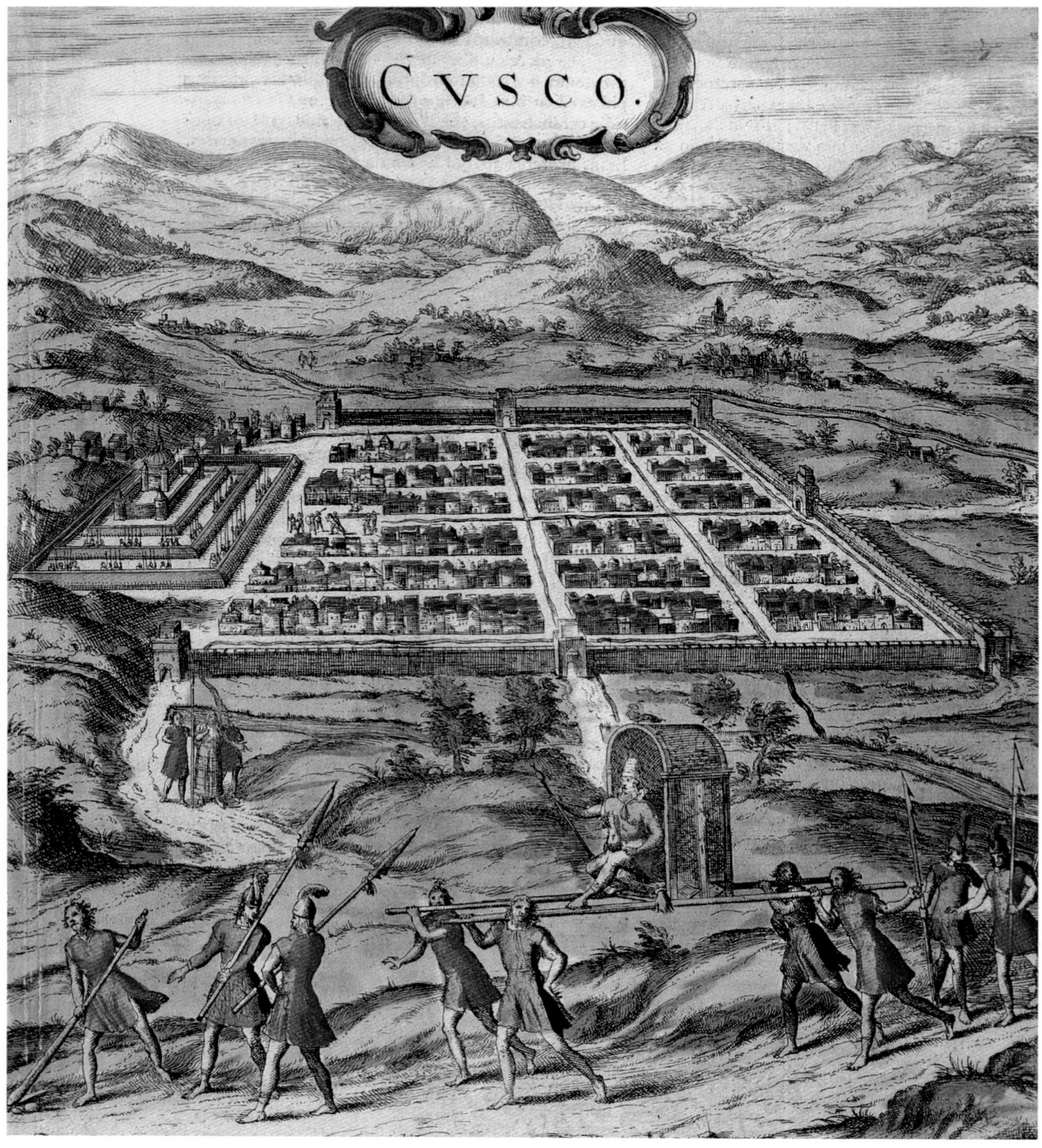

OPPOSITE
Mount Potosí in Peru is portrayed as a conflation of the Virgin Mary and Pachamama (Earth Mother) in this 18th-century painting. The seemingly harmonious blend of native and foreign symbolism belies the fact that the Spanish were making a fortune from silver mines in which many Andean peoples lost their lives.

a huge ransom of gold and silver for his release. But then, in 1533 or 1534, they killed him anyway. The Inca, already divided by the civil war, took sides with or against the Spanish intruders, while many subject peoples of the empire readily joined the newcomers to overthrow the Inca tyranny. Cuzco fell in 1534, the moment that conventionally marks the end of the Inca empire.

However, the Spanish conquest of Peru did not occur quickly, as is often supposed. Many battles were fought, including between the forces of Pizarro and Almagro, who disputed rights of conquest. The Spanish success was due less to armor, swords, and cannon and more to disease and discord among the native peoples.

Although the first conquistadors were few in number, they were the thin edge of a wedge of hundreds of Europeans who subsequently reinforced them—a consideration that may not have occurred to the inhabitants of the Inca realm, preoccupied as most of them were with local affairs. Native resistance continued for decades, with a major uprising in the eighteenth century; even some rebellions in the twentieth century called for restoration of the Inca empire. But this was not to be. A *pachacuti* was under way—a great overturning of an old world—and few of those enmeshed in the Andean struggles of the sixteenth century knew what was to come.

BRAVE NEW WORLD

The turmoil of the early Colonial Period was generally a catastrophe for native peoples, but for some individuals and groups it was a time of opportunity. Spanish colonists who arrived literally in rags amassed huge fortunes—and sometimes lost them again: one conquistador was awarded the great gold sun disk that had hung in the Coricancha, but gambled it away in a late-night card game, giving rise to an expression, "to gamble the sun before dawn." Inca princes were to be found among street sweepers a few years after the conquest, while the allies of the Spanish, such as the Cañari of Ecuador, were awarded lands and special privileges.

The Spanish brought new technologies and a host of new animals, such as horses, cattle, and goats, together with plants such as wheat and barley. But they were soon eating potatoes and "Indian corn," or maize. The conquerors naturally attempted to impose their own laws, customs, and religion, but the native peoples did not simply submit to them. They quickly adapted to using the Spanish courts to fight for their rights and sometimes they were successful. Whenever possible they were selective in the customs they adopted, retaining as many of their own as they could. Andean natives were used to having foreign gods forced upon them—the Inca, after all, had imposed their own deities on their subjects just as forcefully as the Spanish. Andean

peoples took Catholicism and interpreted it through their own ideologies, so that the result was a form of "Andean Catholicism" that retained many old traditional beliefs. Rather than simply capitulating to European ways and ideas, Andean peoples adopted some things and blended and hybridized others.

For centuries since the arrival of the Spanish, Peru and the other Andean countries have been occupied by two distinct cultures, one of European origin and another of native origin. The former culture has usually exploited the latter. In recent decades, however, a new appreciation of the prehistoric, pre-conquest legacy has been underway in these lands. Ever more people are becoming aware that, from the high plains and chilly mountain valleys to the barren coastal deserts, ancient Andeans had struggled in harsh conditions not merely to survive but to build one of the world's great cultural traditions. This tradition produced spectacular feats of engineering and glorious works of art, many of which survive today for the appreciation of present and future generations. In their tenacity and creativity, it is surely the people of the Andes who comprise the region's greatest treasure.

ABOVE
Anyone going through this archway on Taquile Island, Lake Titicaca, passed beneath the cross and the gaze of local officials sculpted in stone. The Spanish made determined efforts to keep their new subjects in check. Nonetheless, native peoples and their culture have endured to the present.

GLOSSARY

Note: Ancient Andeans had no written language so spellings vary; some alternates are provided herewith (in brackets) when they differ greatly. Quechua and Aymara are the major languages currently spoken in the central Andes (increasingly, many scholars are referring to "Inca" instead of Quechua). Because we rarely know terms from pre-contact times and because the Incas were the rulers of the central Andes in the sixteenth century, unless specified otherwise the terms listed are from Quechua. The singular form sometimes also forms the plural (pl.)—for example, Inca, *khipu*, etc. Many scholars follow this practice, although some add an "s."

---

aclla (pl. *acllacuna*) A "Chosen Woman" selected by officials to live chastely and serve the state, particularly through acts of worship, making festival food, *chicha*, and *qompi*, and by becoming a bride for Inca political purposes. She lived in an isolated, sheltered building called an *acllahuasi*. A high-ranking *aclla* was a *mamacona*.

altiplano Spanish for "high plain"—an elevated, broad tableland; in South America it almost always is a reference to the *altiplano* of Bolivia.

anden Spanish for "platform" or "terrace," the great number of which prompted the Spanish to refer to the hills with this term; the name was transformed to "Andes," which we now use for the mountain chain.

apu The mountains and the ancestral mountain deities.

audiencia Spanish for "tribunal court," used in reference to U-shaped, audience hall structures at Chimú administrative centers, particularly at Chan Chan.

ayllu In modern times, a number of unrelated families living in a defined area and following common rules and leaders. The composition and nature of ancient *ayllu*s are uncertain but likely followed similar patterns.

camelid A generic term used in the Americas to refer to llamas, alpacas, vicuñas and guanacos.

ceque An invisible line of sacred power believed to radiate from Cuzco and along which a *huaca* was sited.

chasquis (*caski*) Inca messenger runners organized to run in relays along the Inca roads and stationed in shelter huts (*c'oklya*) spaced at distances of every quarter- or half-league, according to different sources.

chicha A term brought by the Spanish from Central America to refer to native fermented beverages. *Chicha* is called *aqha* in Quechua and was made from various ingredients, notably maize.

chullpa Round or square pre-Inca burial towers often made of fine masonry.

huaca A sacred thing, commonly used to refer to a specific place, often an ancient ruin, and used generically for "mound." *Huaco* was occasionally used to refer to an ancient ceramic vessel.

Huari The city whence arose the empire of the culture known as Wari.

Inca Sometimes spelled Inka, this is the ethnic name of people from a part of the Cuzco region. Historically, the Sapa Inca was the monarch and his principal wife was known as the Coya (Qoya).

Inti The sun god, believed to be the divine ancestor of the Inca dynasty. Specific manifestations and images of the sun were given separate names: "Lord Sun," "Son Sun," and "Brother Sun."

kallanka An Inca great hall, gabled, longer than wide, commonly with one long side pierced by many open entryways. Used as audience chambers, council houses, temporary lodging, and festivals during bad weather.

kero (*quero*) A tumbler-shaped *chicha* drinking vessel. The term has come to be applied to all such shaped vessels, which often were made in pairs. Technically *keros* are of wood while silver and gold versions were *aquilla*.

khipu (*quipu*) Cords on which knots were made by official Inca record keepers (*khipukamayo*). The kind of knot and its placement on a main or pendant cord indicated its numerical value in a decimal system. Accounts were kept and narratives may also have been recorded.

kuraka (*koraka*, *curaca*) An "official," which the Spanish used for Inca government officials and local native lords or leaders. The Caribbean term *cacique* was sometimes used for chiefs and *orejones*, or "big ears," (higher status people wore larger ear spools) for Inca officials.

loma Spanish for "hillock" but used in Peru to refer to fog-fed vegetation and the hills where it thrives, particularly on the central coast.

mitimaes Populations forced by the Inca to resettle in foreign lands, usually because they had resisted conquest or staged a rebellion.

naipes From the Spanish for "playing cards," but used by the Spanish to refer to thin, flat, copper objects which likely were used as a proto-money, especially by late prehistoric cultures on the north coast of Peru.

Nasca A culture centered in the Nazca River valley.

Pachamama "Earth Mother," the Inca Earth goddess.

panaca A royal *ayllu*. *Panaca*s maintained the mummy and the cult of deceased Sapa Incas and they controlled and benefited from his holdings and possessions.

Quechua The "warm valley people" who were neighbors of the Inca and shared their language. When defeated by the Inca's enemies, the Chanka, the Quechua were made "Incas by privilege."

qompi (*cumpi*) The finest Inca cloth, woven from fine wool by *acllacuna* for the exclusive use of Inca royalty. It was finished on both sides and multicolored. A gift of a garment of *qompi* from the Inca was a high honor.

suyu The term for a province of the Inca realm.

tambo (*tampo*) Groups of storehouses and shelters built by the Inca in towns through which roads passed in order to service those traveling on state business.

Tiwanaku (Tiahuanaco) Great Middle Horizon city near Lake Titicaca.

tumi a semicircular-bladed ceremonial knife typical of the Sicán and Lambayeque cultures.

uncu An Inca man's tunic. Usually, a rectangular cloth, folded and sewn at its sides with openings left for arms and neck. The poncho is a post-conquest garment.

BIBLIOGRAPHY

GENERAL

Berrin, Kathleen. (ed.) *The Spirit of Ancient Peru*. Thames and Hudson: London, 1997.

Hill Boone, Elizabeth. (ed.) *Andean Art at Dumbarton Oaks*. Volumes 1 and 2. Dumbarton Oaks Research Library and Collection: Washington, D.C., 1996.

Longhena, Maria and Alva, Walter. *Splendours of the Ancient Andes*. Thames and Hudson: London, 1999.

Morris, Craig and Von Hagen, Adriana. *The Inca Empire and Its Andean Origins*. Abbeville Press: New York, 1993.

Moseley, Michael E. *The Incas and their Ancestors*. Thames and Hudson: London, 2001.

Richardson III, J.B. *People of the Andes*. St. Remy Press/ Smithsonian Books: Montreal/Washington, D.C., 1994.

Silverman, Helaine. (ed.) *Andean Archaeology*. Blackwell Publishers: Oxford, 2004.

Stone-Miller, Rebecca. *Art of the Andes: From Chavin to Inca*. Thames and Hudson: London, 1995.

Stone-Miller, Rebecca. *To Weave for the Sun: Ancient Andean Textiles*. Thames and Hudson: London, 1992.

Von Hagen, Adriana and Morris, Craig. *The Cities of the Ancient Andes*. Thames and Hudson: London, 1998.

1 BEGINNINGS

Donnan, Christopher B. (ed.) *Early Ceremonial Architecture in the Andes*. Dumbarton Oaks Research Library and Collection: Washington, D.C., 1985.

Quilter, Jeffrey. *Life and Death at Paloma: Society and Mortuary Practices at a Preceramic Peruvian Village*. University of Iowa Press: Iowa City, 1989.

Raymond, J. Scott and Burger, Richard L. *The Archaeology of Formative Ecuador*. (eds.) Dumbarton Oaks Research Library and Collection: Washington, D.C., 2003.

2 MONSTER GODS OF THE COSMOS

Burger, Richard L. *Chavin and the Origins of Andean Civilization*. Thames and Hudson: London, 1992.

Paul, Anne. *Paracas Art and Architecture*. University of Iowa Press: Iowa City, 1991.

3 SACRED MOUNTAINS, SACRED PLAINS

Aveni, Anthony F. (ed.) *The Lines of Nasca*. The American Philosophical Society: Philadelphia, 1990.

Bawden, Garth. *The Moche*. Blackwell Publishers: Oxford, 1996.

Pillsbury, Joanne. (ed.) *Moche Art and Archaeology in Ancient Peru*. National Gallery of Art and Yale University Press: New Haven, 2001.

Silverman, Helaine. *Cahuachi in the Ancient Nasca World*. University of Iowa Press: Iowa City, 1993.

Silverman, Helaine and Proulx, Donald. *The Nasca*. Blackwell Publishers: Oxford, 2002.

4 LORDS OF HIGH PLACES

Cook, Anita G. "Wari Art and Society" in Silverman, Helaine. (ed.) *Andean Archaeology*. Blackwell Publishers: Oxford, 2004.

Isbell, William H. and Vranich, Alexi. "The Cities of Wari and Tiwanaku" in Silverman, Helaine. (ed.) *Andean Archaeology*. Blackwell Publishers: Oxford, 2004.

Janusek, John W. "Household and City in Tiwanaku" in Silverman, Helaine. (ed.) *Andean Archaeology*. Blackwell Publishers: Oxford, 2004.

Kolata, Alan L. *The Tiawanaku: Portrait of an Andean Civilization*. Blackwell Publishers: Oxford, 1993.

Shimada, Izumi. (ed.) *Pachacamac: A Reprint of the 1903 Edition by Max Uhle*. University Museum of Archaeology and Anthropology, University of Pennsylvania: Philadelphia, 1991.

5 KINGDOMS OF GOLD

Moseley, Michael E. and Cordy-Collins, Alana. (eds.) *The Northern Dynasties: Kingship and Statecraft in Chimor*. Dumbarton Oaks Library: Washington, D.C., 1990.

Shimada, Izumi. *Pampa Grande and the Mochica Culture*. University of Texas Press: Austin and London, 1994.

6 THE INCA: MASTERS OF THE FOUR QUARTERS

D'Altroy, Terence N. *The Incas*. Blackwell Publishers: Oxford, 2002.

Burger, Richard L. and Salazar, Lucy C. (eds.) *Machu Picchu: Unveiling the Mystery of the Incas*. Yale University Press: New Haven, 2004.

Conrad, Geoffrey W. and Demarest, Arthur A. *Religion and Empire: The Dynamics of Aztec and Inca Expansionism*. Cambridge University Press: Cambridge, 1984.

Quilter, Jeffrey and Urton, Gary. (eds.) *Narrative Threads: Accounting and Recounting in Andean Khipu*. University of Texas Press: Austin and London, 2002.

Rowe, John H. *"Inca Culture at the Time of the Spanish Conquest"* in Steward, Julian. (ed.) *Handbook of South American Indians*, Vol. 2, pp.183–330. Washington D.C., 1946.

7 A WORLD TURNED UPSIDE DOWN

Many of the works of Colonial Period writers such as Bernadbé Cobo, Pedro de Cieza de León, Garcilaso de La Vega, and others have been translated into English and are available at libraries and bookshops.

Cummins, Thomas B.F. *Toasts with the Inca: Andean Abstraction and Colonial Images on Quero Vessels*. University of Michigan Press: Ann Arbor, 2002.

Fane, Diana. (ed.) *Converging Cultures: Art and Identity in Spanish America*. Brooklyn Museum with Harry N. Abrams: New York, 1996.

Salomon, Frank and Urioste, George L. (trans. and eds.) *The Huarochirí Manuscript: A Testament of Ancient and Colonial Andean Religion*. University of Texas Press: Austin and London, 1991.

Silverblatt, Irene. *Moon, Sun, and Witches: Gender Ideologies and Class in Inca and Colonial Peru*. Princeton University Press: Princeton, New Jersey, 1987.

Stern, Steve J. *Peru's Indian Peoples and the Challenge of Spanish Conquest: Huamanga to 1640*. University of Wisconsin Press: Madison, 1982.

INDEX

Note: Page references in *italics* refer to illustration captions and to maps or plans.

ACKNOWLEDGMENTS AND PICTURE CREDITS

Acknowledgments

Sincere thanks are offered by the author to Christopher Westhorp at Duncan Baird, for inviting me to do this project. Peter Bently was a fine editor with whom to work, as was Julia Ruxton, Picture Editor. I offer special thanks to Richard L. Burger and Sarah Quilter who offered very useful commentaries on the draft. Juan Antonio Murro, Assistant Curator; Bridget Gazzo, Pre-Columbian Librarian; Jennifer Younger, Curatorial Assistant; and Kristy Keyes, Assistant to the Director of Studies—all at Dumbarton Oaks—were also of great help in making this book possible and are deeply thanked.

Picture credits

The publisher would like to thank the following people, museums and photographic libraries for permission to reproduce their material. every care has been taken to trace copyright holders. However, if we have omitted anyone we apologize and will, if informed, make corrections to any future edition.

AA = The Art Archive, London
AMNH = American Museum of Natural History, New York
BAL = Bridgeman Art Library, London
DA = Dirk Antrop, Ghent
DO = Dumbarton Oaks Research Library and Collection, Washington, DC
GDO = Gianni Dagli Orti
JBT = John Bigelow Taylor, Highland Falls, New York
JK = Justin Kerr, New York
ML = Museo Arqueológico Rafael Larco Herrera, Lima
MNAA = Museo Nacional de Antropología y Arqueología, Lima
MO = Museo del Oro, Lima
MV = Mireille Vautier, Paris
NGS = National Geographic Society, Washington, DC
SAP = South American Picture, Woodbridge, Suffolk
WFA = Werner Forman Archive, London

(l = left), (r = right), (t = top), (b = bottom)

1 MV/MNAA; **2** Robert Harding Picture Library, London/Loraine Wilson; **3** Corbis/ML/Nathan Benn; **4** JBT/AMNH; **6** JBT/AMNH; **7** ML; **8** SAP/Phillipe Bowles; **10-11** Getty/Stone/Robert Frerck; **13** JBT/AMNH; **14** WFA/Private Collection; **15** Corbis/Nathan Benn; **16** Max Uhle Archive/University of Pennsylvania Museum of Archaeology and Anthropology Museum (neg #84–142518); **17 l** MV/Museum of the Peruvian Culture, Lima; **17 r** MV/Museum of the Peruvian Culture, Lima; **18** DBP archive; **19** Corbis/Nathan Benn; **20–21** AA/GDO; **22** JBT/AMNH; **23** John W Rick, Stanford University; **24** JBT/AMNH; **25** AA/La Condamine School Quito Ecuador/GDO; **27 t** Julio Donoso, Santiago, Chile; **27 b** Corbis/Sygma/Julio Donoso; **28** Yoshio Onuki, University of Tokyo; **29** JBT/AMNH; **30** DA/Museo Arqueológico de la Universidad Nacional, Trujillo; **31 t** AA/Museo Banco Central de Quito/GDO; **32** BAL/Giraudon; **33** MV; **34–35** MV/MNAA; **36** MV; **37** MV; **38** AA/GDO; **41** JK/DO; **42** WFA/courtesy David Bernstein Collection, New York; **43** JK/DO; **44** NGS/William A Allard; **45** JK/DO; **46** AA/MNAA/GDO; **47** SAP/Tony Morrison; **48** JK/DO; **49** AA/MNAA/GDO; **50** AA/MNAA/GDO; **51** JBT/AMNH; **52–53** ML; **54** Peabody Museum, Harvard University photo T1363/Hillel Burger; **55** Corbis/Yann Arthus-Bertrand; **56** JK/DO; **57** AA/Museo Arqueológico Regional, Ica/GDO; **58 b** AA/MNAA/GDO; **58 t** MV/MNAA; **60–61** JBT/AMNH; **62** WFA/courtesy David Bernstein Collection, New York; **63** WFA/courtesy David Bernstein Collection, New York; **64–65** Impact Photos, London/Yann Arthus-Bertrand; **66** AA/National Museum of World Cultures, Gothenburg/GDO; **67** AA/MO/GDO; **68–69** Stephane Compoint, Paris; **70** Christie's Images, London; **71** AA/MNAA/GDO; **72–73** JK/DO; **73 t** JBT/AMNH; **74** AA/MNAA/GDO; **75** Stephane Compoint, Paris; **76–77** Impact Photos, London/Yann Arthus-Bertrand; **77 t** Stephane Compoint, Paris; **78** MV; **79** White Star, Vercelli/Massimo Borchi; **80–81** Corbis/Nathan Benn; **82** Robert Harding Picture Library/ML/Robert Frerck; **83** JK/DO; **84** BAL/British Museum, London; **85** SAP/Tony Morrison; **86** AA/MNAA/GDO; **87** AA/MO/GDO; **88** Corbis/Metropolitan Museum of Art, New York/The Michael C Rockefeller Memorial Collection, Bequest of Nelson A Rockefeller/Nathan Benn; **89** Corbis/Nathan Benn; **90** Corbis/ML/Nathan Benn; **92** DA/Museo del Banco Central de Reserva, Lima; **93** DA/Museo Arqueológico Regional., Huaraz; **94** AA/MNAA/GDO; **95** AKG-images/Private Collection, Lima/Veintimilla; **96** MV; **98** Peabody Museum, Harvard University photo T1361/Hillel Burger; **99** DA/Museo Arqueológico de la Universidad Nacional San Antonio de Abad del Cusco; **100–101** SAP/Tony Morrison; **102** NGS/Museo de Metales Preciosos Precolombino, La Paz/Kenneth Garrett; **103** MV; **104** MV; **105** WFA/Museum für Volkerkunde, Berlin; **106–107** NGS/Kenneth Garrett; **108** JBT/Hoover Institute, Stanford University; **110** DA/Museo Preistorico ed Etnografico "Luigi Pigorini", Rome; **111** JBT/AMNH; **113** NGS/Kenneth Garrett; **114** JK/DO; **115 t** NGS/Kenneth Garrett; **115 b** Corbis/Brian A Vikander; **116** AA/ML/J Enrique Molina; **117** JK/DO; **118** WFA; **119** JBT/AMNH; **120** JK/DO; **121** Corbis/Francis G Mayer; **122–123** JK/DO; **124** JK/DO; **125** JBT/AMNH; **126–127** WFA/Private Collection, Dallas; **128 t** Corbis/Stephanie Colasanti; **128 b** JBT/AMNH; **130** Corbis/ Sygma/Julio Donoso; **132–133** AA/MO/GDO; **134** SAP/Tony Morrison; **135** DA/Rautenstrauch-Joest Museum, Cologne, Collection Ludwig; **136** DA/Museo Banco Central de Reserva, Lima; **137** AA/Gabaldoni Collection Lima/GDO; **138** MV/Amano Museum, Lima; **139** MV/Amano Museum, Lima; **140** Corbis/James Sparshatt; **141** MV/MNAA; **143** MV/Museo Brüning, Lambayeque; **144–145** WFA/Dallas Museum of Art; **146** AA/MNAA/GDO; **147** AKG-images/Museo Brüning, Lambayeque; **148** AA/MNAA/GDO; **149** AA/MNAA/GDO; **150** JK/DO; **151** ML; **152 t** Corbis/Roman Soumar; **152 b** JBT; **153** JK/DO; **155 t** MV; **155 b** AA/Dagli Orti; **156** MV; **157** AA/Dagli Orti; **158** Corbis/Sygma/Julio Donoso; **159** AA/MO/GDO; **160** WFA/Museum für Volkerkunde, Berlin; **161** WFA/ML; **162** BAL/Private Collection; **163** AA/MO/GDO; **164** AA/MO/GDO; **165** JBT/AMNH; **166–167** AA/MO/GDO; **168–169** AA/GDO; **170** BAL/British Museum, London; **171** MV/University of Cuzco Museum; **172** AA/GDO; **173** MV/Pedro de Osma Museum, Lima; **174** BAL/British Museum, London; **175 b** MV; **175 t** SAP/Tony Morrison; **176–177** AA/GDO; **178** JBT/AMNH; **179 t** John Warburton-Lee, Sleaford, Lincs; **179 b** Suzanne Tuhrim, London; **180** John Warburton-Lee, Sleaford, Lincs; **181** WFA/Museum für Volkerkunde, Berlin; **182** MV/MNAA; **183** WFA/Museum für Volkerkunde, Berlin; **184** WFA/Museum für Volkerkunde, Berlin; **185** NGS/Maria Stenzel; **186** AA/GDO; **189 t** Corbis/James Sparshatt; **189 b** Axiom, London/Chris Caldicott; **190** MV; **192–193** AA/GDO; **194** JK/DO; **195** John Warburton-Lee, Sleaford, Lincs; **196** JK/DO; **197** GDO; **198** AA/MO/Dagli Orti; **199** Peabody Museum, Harvard University photo T1355/Hillel Burger; **200** JK/DO; **201** Dr Johan Reinhard/Mountain Institute, Washington DC; **202** DA/Museo de América, Madrid; **203** DA/Museo de América, Madrid; **204–205** AA/GDO; **206–207** MV/Collecion Chavez Ballón, Cuzco; **208** AA/Museo Pedro de Osma Lima/MV; **209** Corbis/Jeremy Horner; **210** MV/Collecion Chavez Ballón, Cuzco; **211** WFA/Museum für Volkerkunde, Berlin; **212** AA/Biblioteca Nacional Madrid/ GDO; **213** AA/Casa de Moneda, Potosi/MV; **215** John Warburton-Lee, Sleaford, Lincs